Fish

BLOOMSBURY KITCHEN LIBRARY

Fish

Bloomsbury Books
London

This edition published 1994 by Bloomsbury Books,
an imprint of The Godfrey Cave Group,
42 Bloomsbury Street, London, WC1B 3QJ.

ISBN 1 85471 512 7

Printed and bound in Great Britain.

Contents

Sea Bass with 20 Cloves of Garlic

Serves 4

Working time: about 20 minutes

Total time: about 1 hour

Calories
200
Protein
23g
Cholesterol
45mg
Total fat
10g
Saturated fat
1g
Sodium
210mg

600 g	sea bass steaks (or halibut)	1¼ lb
2 tbsp	safflower oil	2 tbsp
2	sweet red peppers, diced	2
20	garlic cloves, very thinly sliced	20
1	fresh hot green chili pepper, seeded and finely chopped	1

6 tbsp	finely chopped fresh coriander, plus several whole sprigs for garnish	6 tbsp
¼ tsp	salt	¼ tsp
	freshly ground black pepper	
1 tsp	paprika, preferably Hungarian	1 tsp
½ litre	fish stock or dry white wine	16 fl oz

Rinse the fish under cold running water and pat it dry with paper towels. Remove any scales from the skin; if the steaks are large, cut them in half lengthwise.

Heat the oil over medium heat in a heavy frying pan large enough to hold the fish in one layer. Add the red pepper and sauté it lightly for 2 minutes. Add the garlic, green chili and chopped coriander; reduce the heat to low and cook, stirring frequently, for 1 minute. Place the fish on top of the vegetables and sprinkle it with the salt, some pepper and the paprika. Pour in the stock or wine and bring the liquid to a simmer, basting the fish occasionally. Cover, and reduce the heat to low. Cook until the fish is opaque – about 8 minutes.

With a slotted spoon, transfer the fish to a deep platter. Remove the skin from the steaks. Cover the platter with aluminium foil to keep the fish from drying out while you finish the sauce.

Boil the liquid in the pan, stirring occasionally, until only about 12.5 cl (4 fl oz) remain – 5 to 10 minutes. Pour the sauce over the fish. Serve at room temperature or cold, garnished with the coriander sprigs.

Suggested accompaniments: green salad; bread rolls.

Pike with Onions, Cabbage and Apple

Serves 6

Working time: about 25 minutes

Total time: about 1 hour

Calories 200
Protein 18g
Cholesterol 50mg
Total fat 6g
Saturated fat 2g
Sodium 145mg

1.5 kg	whole pike (or carp)	3 lb	¼ tsp	caraway seeds	¼ tsp
1 tbsp	safflower oil	1 tbsp	¼ tsp	salt	¼ tsp
3	onions, thinly sliced	3		freshly ground black pepper	
250 g	cabbage, thinly sliced	8 oz	1	red apple, cored and cut into wedges	1
¼ litre	dry white wine	8 fl oz	25 g	unsalted butter	¾ oz
1 tbsp	cider vinegar	1 tbsp	1 tbsp	finely cut chives	1 tbsp

To loosen the scales of the pike, scald the fish: put it in the sink or a large basin and pour a kettle of boiling water over it. Scale and clean the fish. Cut off and discard the head.

Preheat the oven to 230°C (450°F or Mark 8). Heat the oil in a large, heavy frying pan over medium-high heat. Add the onions and sauté them until they are translucent – about 4 minutes. Add the cabbage, white wine, cider vinegar, caraway seeds, salt and some pepper, and stir well. Bring the liquid to the boil, then reduce the heat to medium and simmer the mixture for 10 minutes.

Transfer the vegetable mixture to a baking dish large enough to accommodate the pike. Set the pike on top of the vegetables and arrange the apple wedges around it. Bake the fish until the flesh is opaque and feels firm to the touch – about 20 minutes.

Transfer the pike and the apples to a heated serving platter and cover them with aluminium foil; set the platter aside while you finish cooking the cabbage and onions. Return the cabbage-and-onion mixture to the frying pan and cook it over high heat until only about 4 tablespoons of liquid remain – approximately 10 minutes. Add the butter and stir until it melts. Place the vegetables round the fish on the serving platter, sprinkle the chives over the fish and serve immediately.

Suggested accompaniments: rice pilaff; broad beans.

Marinated Pike with Cabbage Salad

Serves 4

Working time: about 30 minutes

Total time: about 2 hours and 45 minutes

Calories 400

Protein 45g

Cholesterol 125mg

Total fat 12g

Saturated fat 4g

Sodium 370mg

1.5 kg	pike (or carp)	**3 lb**
	Marinade	
3 tbsp	clear honey	**3 tbsp**
2 tbsp	low-sodium soy sauce or shoyu	**2 tbsp**
1 tsp	whole grain mustard	**1 tsp**
¼ tsp	cayenne pepper	**¼ tsp**
1 tbsp	tomato paste	**1 tbsp**
1 tsp	finely grated fresh ginger root	**1 tsp**
1	garlic clove, crushed	**1**
4 tbsp	dry white wine	**4 tbsp**
1	orange, rind only, finely grated	**1**
3 tbsp	orange juice	**3 tbsp**
	Cabbage Salad	
350 g	white cabbage	**12 oz**
1 tbsp	virgin olive oil	**1 tbsp**
1	lemon, rind only, finely grated	**1**
1 tbsp	lemon juice	**1 tbsp**
½ tsp	caraway seeds	**½ tsp**
½ tsp	salt	**½ tsp**
	freshly ground black pepper	

Carefully fillet the pike. Remove the skin from the fillets. Cut the fillets into neat 2.5 cm (1 inch) cubes, removing any small bones that you find.

Put all the ingredients for the marinade into a large bowl amd mix them together. Add the pike cubes to the marinade, stir well until the cubes are evenly coated, then cover and leave the fish to marinate for 2 to 3 hours.

Thirty minutes before cooking the pike, make the salad. Cut the cabbage into very fine shreds. In a bowl, mix together the olive oil, lemon rind and juice, caraway seeds, salt and pepper. Add the cabbage to this dressing and mix well.

Spoon the dressed salad into a shallow serving dish, cover the dish, and set it aside until ready to serve.

Preheat the grill. Remove the pike cubes from the marinade and thread the pieces on to wooden skewers. Cook under a hot grill for 4 to 5 minutes until the pike is cooked, turning the skewers half way through cooking. Do not overcook the pike because it will dry out. Arrange the skewers on top of the salad and serve at once.

Suggested accompaniment: tomato salad.

Lemon Sole on a Bed of Mushrooms and Spinach

Serves 4

Working (and total) time: about 35 minutes

Calories 210
Protein 27g
Cholesterol 75mg
Total fat 10g
Saturated fat 1g
Sodium 305mg

500 g	lemon sole fillets, skinned	**1 lb**
350 g	mushrooms, wiped clean and sliced	**12 oz**
500 g	fresh spinach, washed and stemmed, or 300 g (10 oz) frozen spinach, thawed	**1 lb**

1	lemon, juice only	**1**
	freshly ground black pepper	
2 tbsp	safflower oil	**2 tbsp**
1	onion, finely chopped	**1**
⅛ tsp	grated nutmeg	**⅛ tsp**
¼ tsp	salt	**¼ tsp**

Put the mushrooms in a saucepan with the lemon juice and a generous grinding of pepper. Pour in enough water to cover them, and bring the liquid to boil. Reduce the heat to medium and simmer the mixture until the mushrooms are tender – about 5 minutes. Set the pan aside.

Put the fresh spinach, with water still clinging to its leaves, in a large pan over medium heat. Cover the pan and steam the spinach until the leaves are wilted – 2 to 3 minutes. (Frozen spinach needs no cooking.) Squeeze the moisture from the spinach and chop it coarsely.

Heat 1 tablespoon of the oil in a large, heavy frying pan over medium heat. Add the onion and cook it until it is translucent – about

4 minutes. Drain the mushrooms and add them to the pan, then stir in the spinach and cook for 2 minutes. Season the mixture with the nutmeg, salt and some pepper, then spread it evenly in the bottom of a fireproof baking dish.

Preheat the grill. Rinse the fillets under cold running water and pat them dry with paper towels. Fold the fillets into three and lay them on the vegetable mixture. Brush with the remaining oil and grill until the flesh flakes easily when tested with a fork – about 5 minutes. Serve immediately.

Suggested accompaniment: boiled new potatoes.

Sole Fillets with Wine and Grape Sauce

Serves 4
as a starter

Working
(and total)
time: about
40 minutes

Calories
250

Protein
23g

Cholesterol
130mg

Total fat
10g

Saturated fat
4g

Sodium
155mg

2	Dover soles (about 750 g 1½ lb each)	2	175 g	green grapes, halved, seeds removed	6 oz
30 cl	fish stock	½ pint	2 tbsp	double or single cream	2 tbsp
15 cl	dry white wine	¼ pint			
15 g	unsalted butter, softened	½ oz		**Garnish**	
15 g	flour	½ oz	60–90 g	black grapes	2–3 oz

Skin and fillet the soles. With the skinned side on the inside, fold each fillet neatly into three.

Place the fillets in a shallow saucepan in a single layer, then pour in the fish stock. Cover the saucepan and simmer the fillets for 5 to 6 minutes, until they are just cooked.

With a slotted spoon, carefully lift the fillets from the saucepan on to paper towels to drain, then arrange them on a warm serving dish. Cover and keep warm while making the sauce.

Boil the fish stock rapidly until it is reduced to 15 cl (¼ pint), then add the white wine. In a small bowl, blend the butter and flour together to make a smooth paste. Using a whisk, incorporate the butter into the stock a little at a time. Continue to stir the sauce with the whisk until it comes to the boil. Reduce the heat to low, add the green grapes and simmer the sauce for 3 to 4 minutes.

Stir the cream into the sauce and heat through for 1 minute, without boiling. Spoon the sauce over the poached sole fillets, garnish with the black grapes and serve immediately.

Suggested accompaniments: mange-tout; steamed rice.

Dover Sole with Orange and Herbs

Serves 2	**Calories** 170
Working time: about 20 minutes	**Protein** 25g
Total time: about 50 minutes	**Cholesterol** 100mg
	Total fat 5g
	Saturated fat 2g
	Sodium 320mg

1	Dover sole (750 g to 1 kg/1½ to 2 lb), cleaned	**1**
1	large orange, peeled, all pith removed, cut into thin slices	**1**
1 tbsp	mixed chopped fresh herbs (parsley, chives, chervil and dill)	**1 tbsp**

15 g	unsalted butter, melted	**½ oz**
¼ tsp	salt	**¼ tsp**
	freshly ground black pepper	
	sprigs of fresh herbs for garnish	
	grated orange rind	

Preheat the oven to 200°C (400°F or Mark 6).

Remove both black and white skin from the sole. Cut off the head and remove any remaining viscera. Using kitchen scissors, cut away the fins from each side of the sole. Rinse the fish under cold running water, then pat it dry with paper towels.

Lightly butter a large shallow ovenproof dish and place the sole in the dish. Arrange the orange slices in a neat overlapping row down the centre of the fish.

Pour the melted butter over the sole, then sprinkle the top with the chopped herbs, and season with salt and pepper. Cover the dish with foil and cook the sole in the oven for 25 to 30 minutes, until the flesh flakes easily.

Garnish the sole with herb sprigs and grated orange rind. Serve immediately.

Sea Bass Fillets with Anise and Mustard Seeds

Serves 4

Working time: about 15 minutes

Total time: about 25 minutes

Calories 190
Protein 22g
Cholesterol 60mg
Total fat 9g
Saturated fat 4g
Sodium 230mg

2	skinned sea bass fillets (or Norway haddock), about 250 g (8 oz) each, cut in half on the diagonal	2
1	shallot, finely chopped	1
2 tsp	aniseeds or fennel seeds	2 tsp
1 tbsp	mustard seeds	1 tbsp
30 g	dry breadcrumbs	1 oz

2 tsp	fresh thyme, or ½ tsp dried thyme	2 tsp
	freshly ground black pepper	
30 g	unsalted butter	1 oz
1	garlic clove, very finely chopped	1
½	lemon, juice only	½
¼ tsp	salt	¼ tsp

Preheat the oven to 240°C (475°F or Mark 9). Lightly butter the bottom of a heavy, shallow baking dish. Sprinkle the chopped shallot into the dish.

Crack the aniseeds or fennel seeds and the mustard seeds with a mortar and pestle, or on a cutting board with the flat of a heavy knife. Transfer the seeds to a wide, shallow bowl or pan, and combine them with the breadcrumbs, thyme and some pepper. Put the butter and garlic into a saucepan and melt the butter.

Rinse the fillets under cold running water and pat them dry with paper towels. Rub the fillets with the lemon juice and sprinkle them with the salt and some pepper. Brush a fillet on both sides with some of the garlic butter, then coat it well with the breadcrumb mixture and lay it on the shallot in the baking dish. Repeat these steps with the remaining fillets. Dribble any remaining garlic butter over the top.

Bake the fish until it feels firm to the touch and the coating is golden-brown – 10 to 12 minutes. Serve immediately.

Suggested accompaniments: tomato salad; green beans.

Crisp Baked Bream with Tomato and Mint

Serves 4

Working time: about 25 minutes

Total time: about 40 minutes

Calories 280

Protein 22g

Cholesterol 60mg

Total fat 15g

Saturated fat 3g

Sodium 210mg

4	sea bream (or perch or trout), about 250 g (8 oz) each, dressed	4
12.5 cl	skimmed milk	4 fl oz
1	egg white, beaten	1
45 g	cornmeal	$1\frac{1}{2}$ oz
20 g	blanched almonds, chopped	$\frac{3}{4}$ oz
30 g	fresh mint, chopped	1 oz
1	spring onion, trimmed and thinly sliced	1

	freshly ground black pepper	
1 tbsp	safflower oil	1 tbsp
15 g	unsalted butter	$\frac{1}{2}$ oz
$\frac{1}{4}$ tsp	salt	$\frac{1}{4}$ tsp
2	large ripe tomatoes, skinned, seeded and finely chopped	2
1 tbsp	fresh lime or lemon juice	1 tbsp
1 tbsp	red wine vinegar	1 tbsp

Rinse the dressed bream under cold running water and pat them dry. Mix the milk and egg white in a shallow bowl. Soak the fish in this mixture for 15 minutes, turning them twice. Preheat the oven to 180°C (350°F or Mark 4).

While the fish are soaking, combine the cornmeal, almonds, half the mint, the spring onion and a generous grinding of black pepper in a shallow dish. At the end of the soaking time, dredge each fish in the cornmeal to coat it evenly.

Heat the oil and butter in a large, shallow fireproof casserole (preferably one with a non-stick surface) over medium heat. Add the fish and cook them on the first side for 4 minutes. Sprinkle

the fish with $\frac{1}{8}$ teaspoon of the salt and turn them over; sprinkle them with the remaining salt and cook them on the second side for 2 minutes. Put the casserole in the oven for 15 minutes to finish cooking the fish.

While the fish are baking, make the sauce: combine the tomatoes, the remaining mint, the lime or lemon juice, the vinegar and some pepper in a bowl.

When the fish are done, transfer them to a serving platter; pass the sauce seperately.

Suggested accompaniment: corn on the cob.

Monkfish with Artichoke Ragout

Serves 4

Working time: about 40 minutes

Total time: about 1 hour

Calories 260

Protein 21g

Cholesterol 40mg

Total fat 8g

Saturated fat 1g

Sodium 430mg

500 g	monkfish fillets	**1 lb**
4 tbsp	distilled white vinegar	**4 tbsp**
4	globe artichokes	**4**
1½ tbsp	virgin olive oil	**1½ tbsp**
1	onion, finely chopped	**1**
4	garlic cloves, chopped	**4**
¼ litre	red wine	**8 fl oz**

1.25 kg	ripe tomatoes, skinned, seeded and chopped, or 800 g (28 oz) canned, chopped, juice reserved	**2½ lb**
6	oil-cured black olives, stoned and halved	**6**
½ tsp	capers	**½ tsp**
1	bay leaf	**1**

Pour 5 cm (2 in) water into a pan. Add the vinegar.

Break or cut the stalk off one artichoke. Snap off and discard the outer leaves, starting at the base and continuing until you reach the pale yellow leaves at the core. Cut the top two thirds off. Shave off any dark green leaf bases that remain on the bottom. Cut the bottom into quarters; trim away any purple leaves and the fuzzy choke. Cut each quarter into 4 wedges and drop into the vinegar water. Repeat for other artichokes.

Simmer the artichokes until they are tender – about 15 minutes. Drain and set aside.

Rinse the fillets and pat dry; slice into pieces 4 cm (1½ inches) wide. Pour the oil into a heavy

frying pan over high heat. Add the monkfish pieces and sear them for 1 minute on each side. Transfer the fish to a plate and set it aside.

Reduce the heat to medium and cook the onion until translucent – about 4 minutes. Add the garlic and cook for 1 minute. Add the wine and cook it until almost no liquid remains. Stir in the tomatoes, olives, capers and bay leaf. Boil until reduced by half – 5 minutes.

Put the artichoke in the sauce with the fish on top. Reduce the heat to medium, cover, and cook the fish until opaque and firm – about 10 mins. Transfer fish to a serving dish. Raise the heat to high and cook the sauce for 1 to 2 minutes to thicken it. Transfer the artichokes to the serving dish; pour the sauce over, and serve at once.

Salad of Monkfish and Wild Rice

500 g	monkfish fillets	**1 lb**
¼ litre	fish stock or court-bouillon	**8 fl oz**
4 tbsp	chopped shallots	**4 tbsp**
2	garlic cloves, finely chopped	**2**
1½ tbsp	chopped fresh sage, or 1½ tsp dried sage	**1½ tbsp**
½ tsp	salt	**½ tsp**
	freshly ground black pepper	
250 g	wild rice	**8 oz**

¼ litre	dry white wine	**8 fl oz**
1	lemon, juice only	**1**
175 g	shelled young broad beans, thawed if frozen	**6 oz**
4 tbsp	thinly sliced sun-dried tomatoes	**4 tbsp**
250 g	mange-tout, strings removed, pods cut diagonally in half	**8 oz**
3 tbsp	virgin olive oil	**3 tbsp**

Pour the stock and 45 cl (¾ pint) of water into a large pan. Add 2 tbsp of shallots, half of the garlic and half of the sage, 4 tsp of salt and some pepper; boil. Stir in rice, reduce to low and partially cover. Simmer until the rice has absorbed the liquid and is tender – 40 to 50 mins.

Meanwhile, prepare the poaching liquid. In a sauté pan over medium heat, mix the wine, 12.5 cl (4 fl oz) of water, lemon juice, remaining shallots, garlic and sage, salt and pepper.

Rinse the fillets under cold water, cut into bite-sized pieces. When poaching liquid is hot, reduce heat to low and place fish in the liquid. Poach for 5 minutes until the flesh just flakes.

Transfer fish to a plate. Let it cool slightly, then refrigerate it. Do not discard poaching liquid.

When the rice is done, refrigerate in a bowl. Boil the poaching liquid for 5 minutes to reduce it. Add beans and tomatoes, and cook for 3 minutes. Add mange-tout and cook for 1 minute, stirring; there should be just 2 or 3 tbsps of liquid remaining.

Transfer the vegetables to bowl with the rice. Whisk the olive oil into the reduced liquid and pour over the rice and vegetables. Toss well. Add the fish to the bowl and gently toss the salad once more. Serve at room temperature or chilled.

Indian-Spiced Monkfish

Serves 4

Working time: about 25 minutes

Total time: about 40 minutes

Calories 240

Protein 22g

Cholesterol 45mg

Total fat 10g

Saturated fat 1g

Sodium 420mg

500 g	monkfish fillets	1 lb	½ tsp	cumin seeds	½ tsp
2	lemons, juice only	2	¼ tsp	mustard seeds	¼ tsp
4	garlic cloves, chopped	4	¼ tsp	salt	¼ tsp
1 tbsp	chopped fresh ginger root	1 tbsp	2 tbsp	safflower oil	2 tbsp
2 tbsp	chopped fresh coriander	2 tbsp	1	onion, finely chopped	1
1 tsp	coriander seeds	1 tsp	17.5 cl	plain low-fat yogurt	6 fl oz
1 tsp	ground turmeric	1 tsp	75 g	dry breadcrumbs	2½ oz
1 tsp	dark brown sugar	1 tsp			

In a blender, purée the lemon juice, garlic, ginger, coriander, coriander seeds, turmeric, brown sugar, cumin seeds, mustard seeds and salt. (Alternatively, grind the seasonings by hand in a mortar and pestle, then stir in the lemon juice.)

Heat 1 tablespoon of the oil in a heavy frying pan. Add the onion and cook it until it is translucent – about 4 minutes. Add the spice purée and cook for 3 minutes more. Remove the pan from the heat and set it aside.

Preheat the grill and preheat the oven to 230°C (450°F or Mark 8). Rinse the fish and pat it dry with paper towels. Slice the fillets crosswise into pieces 5 cm (2 inches) wide.

Transfer the contents of the pan to a bowl and mix in the yogurt. Transfer half of this yogurt mixture to a small serving bowl and set it aside. Use the other half of the mixture to coat the fish: dip each piece of fish first in the yogurt, then in the breadcrumbs, covering it completely. Place in a fireproof baking dish.

Dribble the remaining oil over the fish. Grill the fish 7.5 cm (3 inches) below the heat source for about 3 minutes on each side. Transfer the dish to the oven and bake the fish until it feels firm to the touch – approximately 10 minutes. Carefully remove from the dish. Serve with yogurt sauce.

Oven-Steamed Norway Haddock

Serves 6
Working time: about 10 minutes
Total time: about 50 minutes

Calories	235
Protein	39g
Cholesterol	160mg
Total fat	8g
Saturated fat	1g
Sodium	180mg

1.5 kg	Norway haddock (or sea bass or sea trout), cleaned	3 lb
2 tbsp	dry sherry	2 tbsp
2 tsp	cornflour	2 tsp
⅛ tsp	salt	⅛ tsp
5 cm	piece of fresh ginger root, peeled and julienned	2 inch
4	spring onions, trimmed and cut into 5 cm (2 inch) pieces	4
15 g	fresh coriander leaves	½ oz
2 tbsp	low-sodium soy sauce or shoyu	2 tbsp
1 tbsp	Chinese black vinegar or balsamic vinegar	1 tbsp
¼ tsp	sugar	¼ tsp

Combine the sherry, cornflour and salt in a small bowl. Rinse the fish under cold running water and pat it dry with paper towels. Cut four or five diagonal slashes on each side of the fish. Rub the sherry marinade over the fish, inside and out, working some of it into the slashes. Place the fish on the shiny side of a large piece of aluminum foil and let it marinate for at least 15 minutes.

Preheat the oven to 230°C (450°F or Mark 8). Insert a strip of ginger and a piece of spring onion into each slash. Place the remainder in the body cavity. Lay a few coriander leaves on top of the fish; put the remainder in the cavity. Combine the soy sauce, vinegar and sugar, and pour over the fish. Fold the foil over the fish and crimp the edges to seal the package tightly.

Set the foil package on a baking sheet and bake the fish until its flesh is opaque and feels firm to the touch – about 25 minutes. Carefully transfer the fish to a warmed serving platter. Pour over any liquid that has collected during baking, and serve immediately.

Suggested accompaniments: stir-fried broccoli and water chestnuts; steamed rice.

Redfish Creole

Serves 6		Calories 220
Working time: about 20 minutes		Protein 21g
Total time: about 30 minutes		Cholesterol 65mg
		Total fat 9g
		Saturated fat 3g
		Sodium 370mg

600 g	redfish fillets (or Norway haddock), the skin left on, cut into 6 equal pieces	**1¼ lb**
20 g	unsalted butter	**¾ oz**
1	small onion, coarsely chopped	**1**
1	sweet green pepper, seeded, deribbed and coarsely chopped	**1**
750 g	ripe tomatoes, skinned, seeded and coarsely chopped, or 400 g (14 oz) canned whole tomatoes, drained and coarsely chopped	**1½ lb**

1	garlic clove, finely chopped	**1**
12.5 cl	fish stock or water	**4 fl oz**
100 g	okra, thinly sliced	**3½ oz**
3 tbsp	Dijon mustard	**3 tbsp**
2 tbsp	paprika, preferably Hungarian	**2 tbsp**
½ tsp	salt	**½ tsp**
	freshly ground black pepper	
125 g	cooked prawns, peeled and deveined	**4 oz**
60 g	flour	**2 oz**
2 tbsp	safflower oil	**2 tbsp**

To prepare the sauce, first melt the butter in a saucepan over medium heat. Add the onion and green pepper; cook, stirring occasionally, until the onion becomes transparent and begins to turn golden – 4 to 5 minutes. Add the garlic and cook it, stirring, for 30 seconds. Stir in the tomatoes, stock or water, okra, mustard, paprika, ¼ teaspoon of the salt and some black pepper. Bring the mixture to the boil, reduce the heat to medium low and simmer the sauce for 5 minutes. Stir in the prawns and cook the sauce for 1 minute more. Set the saucepan aside.

Rinse the fillets under cold running water and pat them dry with paper towels. Season the fillets with the remaining salt and some black pepper. Place the fish in a polythene bag with the flour and shake the bag to coat the fillets.

Heat the oil in a large, heavy frying pan over medium-high heat. Sauté the fillets in the oil until they are opaque all the way through – approximately 2 minutes per side. Reheat the tomato sauce and pour it into a serving platter. Lay the fillets on top of the sauce and serve.

Mahimahi Stuffed with Chilies and Tomatoes

Serves 6

Working
time: about
40 minutes

Total time:
about
1 hour

Calories
215

Protein
23g

Cholesterol
80mg

Total fat
11g

Saturated fat
3g

Sodium
280mg

750 g	mahimahi fillet (or haddock)	**1½ lb**
2 tbsp	virgin olive oil	**2 tbsp**
3	garlic cloves, thinly sliced	**3**
1–2	small chili peppers, seeded and finely chopped	**1–2**
1	red onion, thinly sliced	**1**
500 g	ripe tomatoes,skinned, seeded	**1 lb**

2	lemons	**2**
½ tsp	salt	**½ tsp**
45 g	fresh parsley, coarsely chopped	**1½ oz**
15 g	unsalted butter	**½ oz**
45 g	almonds, sliced	**1½ oz**

Rinse the fillet under cold running water and pat it dry. Cut a large flap on each side of the centre line of the fillet: holding the knife parallel to the centre line at a flat angle, cut from the middle towards the edge of the fillet. (Take care not to cut all the way through to the edge nor down to the bottom of the fillet.) Set the fish aside.

Preheat the oven to 240°C (475°F or Mark 9).

Pour the oil into a large, heavy frying pan over medium-high heat. Add the garlic and chili peppers and cook for 30 seconds. Add the onion and cook for 2 mins. Add the tomatoes, the juice of one of the lemons and ¼ teaspoon of the salt. Cook, stirring, until tomatoes are soft and almost all the liquid has evaporated – about 10 minutes.

Meanwhile, cut six paper-thin slices from remaining lemon. Rub the juice from the remainder of the lemon over the fish and inside the flaps. Put the fish in an oiled baking dish.

Stir the parsley into the stuffing. Fill flaps on the fillet with stuffing. Close over and arrange the lemon slices on top. Bake until opaque and firm – 20 to 25 minutes.

Just before the fish is done, melt the butter in a frying pan over medium heat. Add the sliced almonds and remaining salt; toast the almonds, stirring, until lightly browned – 2 to 3 minutes. Transfer the fish to a warmed platter and scatter almonds on top before serving.

Fillets of Whiting with Mushroom Sauce

Serves 4

Working (and total) time: about 45 minutes

Calories 320
Protein 35g
Cholesterol 65mg
Total fat 5g
Saturated fat 2g
Sodium 300mg

4	whiting (350 g/12 oz each), filleted and skinned	4	250 g	mushrooms, sliced thinly	8 oz
½ tsp	salt	½ tsp	15 g	unsalted butter	½ oz
	freshly ground black pepper		15 g	flour	½ oz
3 tbsp	lemon juice	3 tbsp	2 tbsp	single cream	2 tbsp
30 cl	fish stock	½ pint	750 g	new potatoes, scrubbed	1½ lb
			2 tbsp	chopped parsley	2 tbsp

Rinse the fillets under cold running water and pat them dry with paper towels. Lay the fillets on a work surface skinned side up, season with half tha salt, some pepper and 1 tablespoon of the lemon juice. Roll each fillet up from head to tail.

Place the fillets in a shallow saucepan, pour in the fish stock, cover the saucepan with a tightly fitting lid and cook gently for 8 to 10 minutes.

Meanwhile, put the potatoes on to boil. Place the sliced mushrooms in a bowl, add the remaining lemon juice and mix together.

Using a slotted spoon, lift the cooked whiting fillets from the saucepan on to paper towels to drain, then arrange neatly on a hot serving dish.

Cover and keep warm while making the sauce.

Boil the fish stock rapidly until it is reduced to about ¼ litre (8 fl oz). Melt the butter in the saucepan, add the flour, then stir in the fish stock. Bring the liquid to the boil, stirring all the time. Add the sliced mushrooms and the remaining salt to the sauce, reduce the heat and simmer for 5 minutes until the mushrooms are softened. Stir the cream into the sauce and heat through for 1 minute.

When the potatoes are cooked but still firm, drain them and cut them into slices. Spoon the mushroom sauce over the whiting fillets, then garnish with the hot sliced potatoes and the chopped parsley.

Barbecued Swordfish with Chili Sauce

Serves 6		Calories 265
Working time: about 30 minutes		Protein 28g
		Cholesterol 55mg
Total time: about 1 hour		Total fat 9g
		Saturated fat 1g
		Sodium 325mg

6	small swordfish steaks (or cod), about 150 g (5 oz) each, 1 to 2 cm (½ to ¾ inch) thick	6	4	large, dried mild chili peppers, stemmed and seeded	4
2 tbsp	fresh thyme, or 2 tsp dried thyme	2 tbsp	30 g	sun-dried tomatoes	1 oz
			17.5 cl	fish stock	6 fl oz
3	garlic cloves, finely chopped	3	12.5 cl	tawny port	4 fl oz
2	lemons, juice only	2	2 tsp	safflower oil	2 tsp

Rinse the steaks under cold running water and pat them dry with paper towels. In a shallow dish large enough to hold the steaks in a single layer, combine the thyme, two thirds of the garlic and the lemon juice. Put the steaks in the dish and marinate them in the refrigerator for 1 hour, turning them once or twice.

Light the charcoal in the barbecue about 40 minutes before serving time. While charcoal is heating, cover the chilis with 1 litre (1¾ pints) of boiling water and soak them for 20 minutes.

Drain the chilies and transfer them to a blender or food processor. Add the tomatoes and stock, and purée the mixture.

Pour the port into a non-reactive saucepan over medium-high heat; bring the port to the boil and cook it until it is reduced by half – 3 to 4 minutes. Stir in the chili-tomato purée and the remaining third of the garlic. Reduce the heat to medium and cook, stirring occasionally, for 5 minutes. Strain it through a fine sieve on to the bottom of a warm serving platter.

When the charcoal is hot, remove the steaks from the marinade and brush them with the oil. Cook the steaks for only 2 to 3 minutes per side – the flesh should be barely opaque. Set the steaks on top of the sauce and serve immediately.

Suggested accompaniments: green salad; pitta bread.

Grilled Swordfish in Apple-Tarragon Sauce

Serves 4

Working time: about 15 minutes

Total time: about 25 minutes

Calories 305
Protein 30g
Cholesterol 60mg
Total fat 10g
Saturated fat 2g
Sodium 290mg

750 g	swordfish steaks (or tuna), trimmed and cut into quarters	**1½ lb**
2 tbsp	safflower oil	**2 tbsp**
2 tbsp	finely chopped shallot	**2 tbsp**
2 tbsp	chopped fresh tarragon, or 2 tsp dried tarragon	**2 tbsp**
12.5 cl	fish stock	**4 fl oz**
4 tbsp	unsweetened apple juice	**4 tbsp**

1½ tsp	cornflour, mixed with 1 tbsp cold water	**1½ tsp**
¼ tsp	salt	**¼ tsp**
	freshly ground black pepper	
1	red apple, quartered, cored and cut into thin wedges	**1**
1	yellow apple, quartered, cored and cut into thin wedges	**1**

Preheat the grill or light the charcoal in the barbecue.

To prepare the sauce, pour 1 tablespoon of the oil into a saucepan over medium heat. Add the shallot and cook it until it is translucent – 1 to 2 minutes. Add the tarragon, stock, apple juice, cornflour mixture, ⅛ teaspoon of the salt and some pepper. Whisking constantly, bring the mixture to the boil and let it thicken. Reduce the heat to low and simmer the sauce for 2 to 3 minutes. Set the pan aside.

Rinse the fish steaks under cold running water and pat them dry with paper towels. Season the steaks with the remaining salt and a generous grinding of pepper, then brush them with the remaining oil. Grill or barbecue the steaks until their flesh is opaque and feels firm to the touch – 3 to 4 minutes per side.

When the fish is nearly done, reheat the sauce over low heat. Serve the steaks immediately, topped with the warm sauce and garnished with the apple slices.

Suggested accompaniment: sautéed yellow squash or courgettes with chopped spring onion tops.

Grayling Gratin

Serves 6

Working time: about 40 minutes

Total time: about 1 hour and 10 minutes

Calories 300

Protein 19g

Cholesterol 45mg

Total fat 9g

Saturated fat 3g

Sodium 170mg

500 g	skinned grayling fillets (or other white fish)	**1 lb**	
1	lemon, juice only	**1**	
	freshly ground black pepper		
1 kg	waxy potatoes, scrubbed	**2 lb**	
1.25 kg	ripe tomatoes, quartered, or 800 g (28 oz) canned whole tomatoes, chopped, juice reserved	**2½ lb**	
1	fresh hot green chili pepper, seeded and chopped	**1**	
2	garlic cloves, finely chopped	**2**	
1 tsp	chopped fresh oregano, or ½ tsp dried oregano	**1 tsp**	

¼ tsp	ground cumin	**¼ tsp**	
¼ tsp	cayenne pepper	**¼ tsp**	
¼ tsp	salt	**¼ tsp**	
1 tbsp	virgin olive oil	**1 tbsp**	
2	onions, thinly sliced	**2**	
	Herbed Topping		
45 g	dry breadcrumbs	**1½ oz**	
2 tbsp	chopped fresh parsley	**2 tbsp**	
¼ tsp	chopped fresh oregano, or ⅛ tsp dried oregano	**¼ tsp**	
⅛ tsp	ground cumin	**⅛ tsp**	
20 g	unsalted butter	**¾ oz**	

Rinse fillets and pat dry. Dribble the lemon juice over. Season with black pepper.

Put potatoes in a pan, with water to cover and boil. Reduce heat and cook until tender – about 15 minutes.

Put the fresh tomatoes in a pan with 12.5 cl (4 fl oz) of water. (If using canned tomatoes, add juice but no water.) Cook, stirring, until soft and most of the liquid has evaporated, – about 20 minutes. Purée through a sieve. Mix with the chili, garlic,

oregano, cumin, cayenne pepper and salt.

Gently fry the onions until golden-brown and soft – about 7 minutes. Add 12.5 cl (4 fl oz) of water to deglaze the pan; stir well and set aside.

Preheat the oven to 230°C (450°F or Mark 8). Peel and cut potatoes into chunks. In a baking dish, mix potatoes with the sauce and onions. Place the fillets on top. Combine breadcrumbs and herbs and sprinkle over fish. Dot with butter. Bake until fish feels firm – about 20 mins.

Skate with Red Pepper and French Beans

Serves 4

Working (and total) time: about 40 minutes

Calories 325
Protein 31g
Cholesterol 60mg
Total fat 10g
Saturated fat 1g
Sodium 275mg

1 kg	skate wings, skinned	**2 lb**	**4 tbsp**	red wine vinegar	**4 tbsp**
½ litre	dry white wine	**16 fl oz**	**2 tbsp**	virgin olive oil	**2 tbsp**
¼ litre	fish stock or water	**8 fl oz**	**1 tbsp**	fresh lemon juice	**1 tbsp**
1	shallot, thinly sliced	**1**	**1**	sweet red pepper, seeded, deribbed and thinly sliced	**1**
2	fresh thyme sprigs, or ¾ tsp dried thyme	**2**	**¼ tsp**	salt	**¼ tsp**
8	whole cloves	**8**		freshly ground black pepper	
4	spring onions, thinly sliced, white parts kept separate from the green	**4**	**150 g**	French beans, trimmed, halved lengthwise diagonally	**5 oz**

Rinse the skate well. In a large, non-reactive frying pan, combine the wine, the stock or water, the shallot, thyme and cloves. Bring to the boil, then reduce the heat to medium-low and put the skate in the liquid. Poach the fish until it is opaque – about 12 minutes.

While the skate is cooking, prepare the vinaigrette: combine the white spring onion slices, the vinegar, oil and lemon juice. Set aside.

When the skate is cooked, transfer it to a plate. Strain the poaching liquid into a bowl, then pour the strained liquid back into the pan. Add the pepper strips, the salt and some pepper,

and cook over medium-low heat for 5 minutes. Add the beans to the pan; cook the vegetables for 5 minutes more.

With a slotted spoon, transfer the vegetables to the bowl containing the vinaigrette. Stir the green spring onion slices into the vegetable mixture. Increase the heat to high and boil the liquid rapidly until it is syrupy – 2 to 3 minutes. Pour the liquid into the vegetable mixture.

With your fingers, lift the skate meat from the cartilage. Put the meat on a platter and arrange the vegetables around it, spooning some of the vinaigrette over the top. Serve warm or cold.

Red Snapper in Saffron Sauce

Serves 4

Working (and total) time: about 30 minutes

Calories
245

Protein
24g

Cholesterol
80mg

Total fat
9g

Saturated fat
4g

Sodium
200mg

500 g	skinned red snapper fillets (or John Dory)	**1 lb**	
¼ tsp	salt	**¼ tsp**	
¼ litre	dry white wine	**8 fl oz**	
1	shallot, chopped	**1**	
1	garlic clove, crushed	**1**	
1	fresh thyme sprig, or ½ tsp dried thyme	**1**	
1 tsp	fennel seeds, crushed	**1 tsp**	
10	black peppercorns, cracked	**10**	
15 g	unsalted butter	**½ oz**	
20	saffron threads, steeped in 4 tbsp hot water for 10 minutes	**20**	
1 tsp	Dijon mustard	**1 tsp**	
4 tbsp	single cream, mixed with ½ tsp cornflour	**4 tbsp**	

Gently rinse the fillets under cold running water and pat them dry with paper towels. Sprinkle the fish with the salt and set it aside.

In a large, heavy frying pan, combine the wine, shallot, garlic, thyme, fennel seeds, peppercorns and butter. Bring the mixture to the boil, then reduce the heat to medium and simmer for 3 minutes. Put the fillets in the liquid and reduce the heat to low. Cover the pan and poach the fish until it is opaque and feels firm to the touch – about 6 minutes. Carefully transfer the fish to a warmed serving dish and cover the fish with aluminium foil to keep it warm.

Increase the heat under the pan to medium-high and reduce the poaching liquid to approximately 12.5 cl (4 fl oz) – about 5 minutes. Strain the liquid into a small saucepan. Pour into the saucepan any juices that have collected on the serving dish, then stir in the saffron mixture and the mustard. Simmer the sauce for 2 minutes. Whisk in the cream-and-cornflour mixture, and cook the sauce until it thickens slightly – about 1 minute more. Pour round the fillets and serve at once.

Suggested accompaniment: boiled new potatoes.

Stir-Fried Shark with Chinese Cabbage

Serves 4

Working time: about 15 minutes

Total time: about 30 minutes

Calories 240
Protein 25g
Cholesterol 45mg
Total fat 9g
Saturated fat 1g
Sodium 355mg

500 g	shark meat (or swordfish or tuna)	1 lb
2 tbsp	low-sodium soy sauce or shoyu	2 tbsp
1 tbsp	dark sesame oil	1 tbsp
1 tbsp	fresh lime juice	1 tbsp
1	bunch spring onions, trimmed, sliced diagonally into 1 cm ($\frac{1}{2}$ inch) pieces, the white parts kept separate from the green	1
2	garlic cloves, finely chopped	2
1 tbsp	orange marmalade or apricot jam	1 tbsp
	freshly ground black pepper	
1$\frac{1}{2}$ tbsp	safflower oil	1$\frac{1}{2}$ tbsp
1	carrot, peeled, halved lengthwise and cut diagonally into thin slices	1
500 g	Chinese cabbage, trimmed and sliced into 2 cm ($\frac{3}{4}$ inch) strips	1 lb

Wash the fish under cold running water and pat it dry with paper towels. Cut it into pieces about 5 cm (2 inches) long and 1 cm ($\frac{1}{2}$ inch) wide. In a large bowl, combine 1 tablespoon of the soy sauce with the sesame oil, lime juice, white spring onion pieces, garlic, marmalade or jam and some pepper. Add the fish pieces to the mixture and let marinate for at least 15 minutes.

In a wok or large frying pan, heat 1 tablespoon of the safflower oil over high heat. Add the carrot and stir-fry them for 1 minute, add the cabbage, all but 1 tablespoon of the green spring onion and the remaining soy sauce. Stir-

fry until the cabbage is barely wilted – about 2 minutes. Transfer the vegetables to a bowl.

Heat the remaining safflower oil in the wok or pan over high heat. Add the marinated fish and gently stir-fry it until it is opaque and feels firm to the touch – approximately 2 minutes. Return the vegetables to the pan and toss them with the fish. Transfer the mixture to a large plate, sprinkle with the reserved green spring onion pieces, and serve.

Suggested accompaniment: fresh Chinese egg noodles.

Prosciutto-Stuffed Plaice with Hot-and-Sour Sauce

Serves 4

Working time: about 30 minutes

Total time: about 1 hour

Calories 145
Protein 21g
Cholesterol 55mg
Total fat 3g
Saturated fat 1g
Sodium 345mg

4	plaice or sole fillets (about 125 g/4 oz each)	4
2 tbsp	rice wine or dry white wine	2 tbsp
4	spring onions, trimmed, the bottom 7.5 cm (3 inches) halved lengthwise, the tops thinly sliced diagonally	4
8	mange-tout, strings removed and halved lengthwise	8
½	sweet red pepper, seeded, deribbed and cut lengthwise into thin strips	½
1	paper-thin slice of prosciutto or other dry-cured ham (about 15 g/½ oz), cut into 8 thin strips	1

Hot-and-Sour-Sauce

1	lemon	1
1 tbsp	rice vinegar	1 tbsp
1 tbsp	low-sodium soy sauce or shoyu	1 tbsp
1 tsp	sweet chili sauce, or ½ tsp crushed dried chili pepper mixed with 1 tsp golden syrup and ½ tsp vinegar	1 tsp
¼ tsp	dark sesame oil	¼ tsp
1 tsp	cornflour, mixed with 2 tsp water	1 tsp
1 tsp	safflower oil	1 tsp
1 tbsp	grated fresh ginger root	1 tbsp
1 tsp	garlic clove, finely chopped	1 tsp

Rinse fish; pat dry. Put in a shallow dish and sprinkle with the wine; marinate in refrigerator for 30 mins.

Next, blanch spring onion bottoms and mange-tout for 10 secs. Drain, refresh. Drain and pat dry.

Lay ¼ of the spring onion bottoms, mange-tout and red pepper and two strips of prosciutto across the centre of each fillet. Roll up and place it seam side down on a plate. Set in a bamboo steamer basket in a wok with 2.5 cm (½ inch) water. (If you lack a steamer, set the plate on a wire rack in a large pan

with 1 cm/½ inch water.) Cover tightly and steam until fish is opaque – about 6 mins.

Grate the rind of the lemon into a bowl. Squeeze the lemon juice into the bowl, add the vinegar, soy sauce, chili sauce, sesame oil and cornflour. Stir. Heat safflower oil and gently fry garlic and ginger for 2 mins. Add vinegar mixture and stir for 1 min to thicken. When fish is done, add liquid from plate to sauce. Serve fish rolls on individual plates with sauce and spring onion garnish.

Halibut Steaks in Peppery Papaya Sauce

Serves 4

Working time: about 25 minutes

Total time: about 40 minutes

Calories 275
Protein 28g
Cholesterol 80mg
Total fat 13g
Saturated fat 5g
Sodium 240mg

4	halibut steaks, total weight 750 g (1½ lb)	4
1 tbsp	safflower oil	1 tbsp
1	papaya (about 500 g/1 lb), peeled, seeded and cut into 2.5 cm (1 inch) pieces	1
1	small onion, coarsely chopped	1
¼ tsp	salt	¼ tsp
12.5 cl	fish stock	4 fl oz
6 tbsp	fresh lime juice	6 tbsp
3 tbsp	double cream	3 tbsp
½	large, dried mild chili pepper, seeded and sliced into paper-thin strips, or ¾ tsp red pepper flakes	½
2	spring onions, trimmed and sliced diagonally into 1 cm (½ inch) pieces	2

Heat the oil in a large, non-reactive frying pan over medium heat. Add the papaya, onion and ⅛ teaspoon of the salt. Cook, stirring frequently, for 7 minutes. Pour in the stock and all but 1 tablespoon of the lime juice. Bring the liquid to the boil, reduce the heat and simmer, partially covered, for 10 minutes. Preheat the grill.

Transfer the papaya mixture to a processor or blender. Purée the mixture until smooth, stopping once to scrape the sides. Put the cream and chili pepper in a saucepan over medium heat. Simmer the cream for 3 minutes, whisking occasionally. Reduce the heat to low and whisk the papaya purée into the cream a spoonful at a time.

Rinse the steaks under cold running water and pat them dry with paper towels. Sprinkle the fish with the remaining salt and the remaining lime juice. Put the steaks in a lightly-buttered shallow, fireproof dish and grill them about 10 cm (4 inches) below the heat source for 4 minutes on the first side. Turn them over, sprinkle them with the sliced spring onions, and continue cooking until the flesh feels firm to the touch and the spring onions are browned – approximately 3 minutes.

Transfer the steaks to a warmed platter and spoon the sauce round them. Serve immediately.

Suggested accompaniment: rice salad.

Poached Halibut with Avocado Sauce

Serves 4

Working (and total) time: about 30 minutes

Calories
310

Protein
36g

Cholesterol
95mg

Total fat
18g

Saturated fat
2g

Sodium
255mg

4	halibut steaks (about 250 g/8 oz each)	**4**
60 cl	court-bouillon	**1 pint**
	Avocado Sauce	
1	large ripe avocado	**1**
½	small fresh green chili pepper, seeded and chopped	**½**

2 tbsp	fresh lime juice	**2 tbsp**
¼ tsp	salt	**¼ tsp**
	freshly ground black pepper	
	Garnish	
1	small lemon, thinly sliced	**1**
1	lime, thinly sliced	**1**
	fresh parsley sprigs (optional)	

Trim the halibut steaks to neaten, then rinse them under cold water. Pat them dry with paper towels.

Pour the court-bouillon into a wide shallow saucepan or fireproof casserole. Place the halibut steaks in the court-bouillon in a single layer, ensuring that they are well covered with liquid. Cover the saucepan and simmer the halibut for 6 to 8 minutes, until the flesh flakes easily.

Meanwhile, cut the avocado in half lengthwise and remove the stone. Carefully peel away the skin, then roughly chop the flesh. Place the avocado in a food processor or blender with the

lime juice, chili pepper, salt and pepper. Blend for 1 minute until very smooth. (Alternatively, the ingredients may be mashed together in a mixing bowl with a fork.) Spoon the sauce into a serving bowl and set aside.

Using a slotted spoon, carefully lift the halibut steaks out of the court-bouillon on to a hot serving dish. Garnish with the sliced lemon and lime and the parsley sprigs, if using. Serve immediately, accompanied by the avocado sauce.

Suggested accompaniment: new potatoes tossed in chives.

Flounder-Stuffed Tomatoes

Serves 6 as an appetizer					Calories 155

Working time: about 35 minutes

Total time: about 45 minutes

Protein 15g
Cholesterol 45mg
Total fat 7g
Saturated fat 2g
Sodium 200mg

500 g	flounder fillets (or plaice or sole)	1 lb	1	large shallot, chopped	1
6	large ripe tomatoes	6	1 tsp	fresh thyme, or ¼ tsp dried thyme	1 tsp
3	carrots, peeled and thinly sliced	3	¼ tsp	salt	¼ tsp
2 tbsp	fresh lemon juice	2 tbsp		freshly ground black pepper	
1½ tbsp	virgin olive oil	1½ tbsp	4 tbsp	single cream	4 tbsp
5	garlic cloves, crushed	5			

Rinse the fillets and pat them dry. Slice crosswise into pieces about 1 cm (½ inch) wide.

Slice the tops off the tomatoes and reserve them. With a spoon, scoop out and discard the seeds and juice. Set the tomatoes upside down on paper towels to drain. Preheat the oven to 200°C (400°F or Mark 6).

Cook the carrots in boiling water with the lemon juice until tender – about 15 mins.

While the carrots are cooking, heat the oil in a large, heavy frying pan over medium heat. Add the garlic cloves and cook them for 2 minutes. Stir in the shallot and cook it for 30 seconds. Add the fish pieces, the thyme, ⅛ teaspoon of the salt and a generous grinding of pepper. Cook the mixture for 10 minutes,

stirring gently with a fork to break up the fish. Stir in the cream and remove the frying pan from the heat. Discard the cloves of garlic

When the carrots are done, drain them, reserving 6 tablespoons of the cooking liquid. In a food processor, blender or sieve, purée the carrots, reserved cooking liquid, the remaining salt and some pepper until smooth. Add the carrot purée to the pan and mix gently; spoon the mixture into the tomato shells.

Put the filled tomato shells in a baking dish and cover them with the reserved tops. Bake the shells until their skins start to crack – about 10 minutes. Remove the shells from the oven and discard the tops. Serve at once.

Seviche of Plaice

			Serves 6 as an appetizer
			Working time: about 30 minutes
			Total time: about 3 hours and 30 minutes

			Calories 110
			Protein 15g
			Cholesterol 40mg
			Total fat 1g
			Saturated fat 0g
			Sodium 170mg

1.5 kg	whole plaice (or sole), boned and filleted, yielding about 500 g (1 lb) of fillets	**3 lb**
4	lemons, halved, the juice and 6 of the empty halves reserved	**4**
5	limes, juice only	**5**
12.5 cl	fresh orange juice	**4 fl oz**
3	hot chili peppers, halved, seeded and thinly sliced crosswise	**3**
2 tbsp	chopped fresh coriander or parsley	**2 tbsp**
1	garlic clove, finely chopped	**1**
2 tbsp	sugar	**2 tbsp**
¼ tsp	salt	**¼ tsp**
	freshly ground black pepper	
18	lettuce leaves, washed and dried	**18**
1	small red onion, thinly sliced, the rings separated	**1**

Rinse the fillets under cold running water and pat them dry with paper towels. Cut the fillets into bite-sized strips about 6 cm (2½ inches) long and 2.5 cm (1 inch) wide; then arrange the fish strips in a single layer in a shallow 20 by 28 cm (8 by 11 inch) glass dish.

In a separate bowl, combine all of the remaining ingredients except the reserved lemon halves, the lettuce and onion. Stir the mixture well and pour it over the fish to just cover. If necessary, add more lemon juice. Cover and refrigerate until the thickest piece of fish, when cut in half, is opaque throughout – about 3 hours.

Cut the edge of each reserved lemon half in a decorative sawtooth pattern. To serve the seviche, spoon some of it into each lemon half. Divide the lettuce between six serving plates. Set a filled lemon half and some of the remaining seviche on the lettuce on each plate, and garnish with the onion rings.

Sole Baked in Parchment

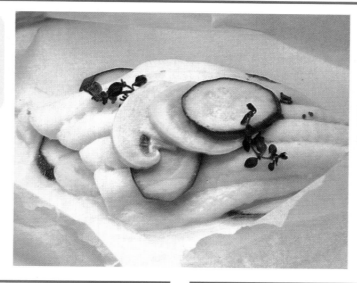

Serves 4

Working time: about 15 minutes

Total time: about 30 minutes

Calories
170
Protein
20g
Cholesterol
70mg
Total fat
8g
Saturated fat
4g
Sodium
275mg

4	sole or plaice fillets, about 125 g (4 oz) each	**4**
2	small courgettes (preferably 1 green and 1 yellow), thinly sliced	**2**
3	large mushrooms, thinly sliced	**3**
4	fresh thyme sprigs, or ½ tsp dried thyme	**4**

4 tbsp	dry vermouth or dry white wine	**4 tbsp**
30 g	unsalted butter, cut into small pieces	**1 oz**
¼ tsp	salt	**¼ tsp**
	freshly ground black pepper	

Preheat the oven to 220°C (425°F or Mark 7). Rinse the fillets under cold running water and pat them dry with paper towels. Using a diagonal lengthwise cut, divide each fillet in half to make one thick and one thin fillet.

Cut four pieces of parchment paper or aluminium foil about 30 by 45 cm (12 by 18 inches). Fold each piece in half lengthwise, cut each piece into a half-heart shape, as you would a valentine. Flatten out and lightly butter each.

Layer one quarter of the fish and vegetables on one half of the heart. Begin with a bed of courgette (but save enough to form a top layer). Place a thick fillet on the courgette bed; top the fillet with the mushrooms. Put a thin fillet on top of the mushrooms, and top it in turn with a final layer of the reserved courgette. To each layered assembly, add a sprig of fresh thyme or a sprinkling of dried thyme, 1 tablespoon of the vermouth or wine, one quarter of the butter, one quarter of the salt and some pepper.

Fold the other ½ of the heart over the layered assembly and bring the cut edges together. Seal by crimping edges together in a series of folds.

Transfer the packages to a baking sheet. Bake them for 10 minutes per 2.5 cm (1 inch) of thickness of the entire assembly – approximately 15 minutes in all.

Put the packages on individual plates; let each diner open his own package.

Suggested accompaniment: pitta bread.

Prawns and Asparagus Wrapped in Sole

Serves 6

Working (and total) time: about 1 hour

Calories 200

Protein 21g

Cholesterol 90mg

Total fat 5g

Saturated fat 2g

Sodium 125mg

3	sole (or plaice), about 600 to 750 g (1¼ to 1½ lb) each	**3**
35 cl	dry white wine	**12 fl oz**
1 tbsp	red wine vinegar	**1 tbsp**
250 g	medium prawns, peeled and deveined, the shells reserved	**8 oz**
150 g	asparagus, sliced diagonally into 5 mm (¼ inch) pieces	**5 oz**
2 tbsp	finely cut fresh dill	**2 tbsp**
3	shallots, finely chopped	**3**
1½ tbsp	fresh lemon juice	**1½ tbsp**
	freshly ground black pepper	
3	ripe tomatoes, skinned, seeded and coarsely chopped	**3**
2 tsp	tomato paste	**2 tsp**

Simmer shells in wine, vinegar and ¼ litre (8 fl oz) of water for 20 minutes.

Meanwhile, fillet the fish. Rinse the fillets, pat dry; set aside.

Strain and discard the shells and pour the liquid back into the pan over medium heat. Add prawns and asparagus, blanch for 30 seconds. Transfer prawns and asparagus to a bowl. Reserve liquid. Add 1 tbsp of dill, half of shallots, lemon juice and some pepper; mix well.

Preheat the oven to 190°C (375°F or Mark 5). With a diagonal crosswise cut, slice one of the thinner fillets in half. Overlap the two halves to form a base, and set in an oiled baking dish. Wrap a larger fillet around base to form a collar,

pin ends together with a tooth pick. Fill with one sixth of the mixture. Repeat with remaining fillets to form six portions.

Cover the dish with foil, its dull side up. Bake until the sole is opaque – about 15 minutes.

Add tomatoes, tomato paste and remaining shallots to the liquid in pan, set over medium-high heat. Stir until reduced to about 30 cl (½ pint) – about 10 minutes. Purée the sauce. Return to the pan and stir in remaining dill. Keep warm. Transfer cooked fish to a serving platter. Whisk butter and some black pepper into the sauce and pour some over the fish, serving the rest separately.

Brill with Curried Tomato Sauce

Serves 4

Working
time: about
20 minutes

Total time:
about
50 minutes

Calories
195
Protein
23g
Cholesterol
60mg
Total fat
6g
Saturated fat
1g
Sodium
215mg

4	brill fillets (or halibut), about 125 g (4 oz) each, rinsed and patted dry	4
1	shallot, finely chopped	1
1	garlic clove, finely chopped	1
$\frac{1}{8}$ tsp	salt	$\frac{1}{8}$ tsp
	freshly ground black pepper	
1 tbsp	dry white wine	1 tbsp
6 tbsp	fish stock or water	6 tbsp
	parsley sprigs	

	Curried Tomato Sauce	
1 tbsp	virgin olive oil	1 tbsp
2	garlic cloves, finely chopped	2
2 tsp	curry powder	2 tsp
1.25 kg	ripe tomatoes, skinned, seeded and finely chopped	2¼ lb
$\frac{1}{8}$ tsp	salt	$\frac{1}{8}$ tsp
	freshly ground black pepper	
2 tsp	tomato paste	2 tsp
1 tbsp	chopped fresh parsley	1 tbsp

Heat the oil in a large pan over low heat. Add the garlic and stir until soft but not browned – 30 secs. Add curry powder and cook for 30 secs more, stirring. Stir in the tomatoes, salt and some pepper, and simmer until the tomatoes are soft – 30 mins. Add the tomato paste, then purée the sauce, return it to the pan and set it aside.

Preheat the oven to 220°C (425°F or Mark 7). Lightly oil a heavy baking dish. Cut a piece of foil to the dimensions of the dish, and oil one side. Sprinkle the shallot and garlic into the dish.

Fold the fillets in half, arrange them in the dish, and season. Pour on the wine and stock. Lay the foil, oiled side down, over the fish. Bake until fish is opaque – 9 mins.

Remove the foil. Carefully transfer the fillets to a serving platter. Re-cover and keep them warm. Strain the cooking liquid into the tomato sauce. Bring to the boil and stir until thickened – 2 mins. Add parsley.

Serve the fish surrounded by sauce, with parsley garnish.

Cod Steak Cooked with Green Pepper and Tomatoes

Serves 4

Working time: about 20 minutes

Total time: about 50 minutes

Calories 195
Protein 32g
Cholesterol 70mg
Total fat 5g
Saturated fat 1g
Sodium 340mg

4	cod steaks (175 to 250 g/6 to 8 oz each)	**4**
1 tbsp	virgin olive oil	**1 tbsp**
1	onion, halved and sliced thinly	**1**
1	large sweet green pepper, seeded, deribbed and sliced thinly	**1**
500 g	tomatoes, skinned, seeded and chopped	**1 lb**
3	garlic cloves, crushed	**3**

2 tsp	mixed fresh herbs (thyme, oregano and rosemary)	**2 tsp**
½ tsp	salt	**½ tsp**
	freshly ground black pepper	

Garnish
fresh thyme sprigs
black olives

Trim the fins from the cod steaks to neaten. Rinse under cold running water, then pat dry with paper towels. Preheat the oven to 200°C (400°F or Mark 6).

Heat the oil in a large frying pan, add the cod steaks and brown them very lightly on both sides. Transfer them to a shallow ovenproof dish.

Add the onion and pepper to the oil remaining in the frying pan. Sauté them gently until softened but not browned. Stir the tomatoes, garlic, herbs and seasoning into the onion and pepper.

Spoon the pepper and tomato mixture over the cod steaks. Cover the dish and cook in the oven for 30 to 35 minutes, until the cod flakes easily.

Garnish the steaks with sprigs of fresh thyme and black olives. Serve immediately.

Cod Fishcakes with Horseradish Sauce

Serves 4

Working time: about 20 minutes

Total time: about 40 minutes

Calories 180
Protein 21g
Cholesterol 105mg
Total fat 4g
Saturated fat 1g
Sodium 490mg

350 g	cod fillets (or haddock or coley)	12 oz		2 tbsp	anise-flavoured liqueur (optional)	2 tbsp
125 g	dry breadcrumbs	4 oz		2 tbsp	fresh lemon juice	2 tbsp
1	egg	1		1½ tsp	capers, drained and chopped	1½ tsp
1	egg white	1		1 tbsp	paprika	1 tbsp
125 g	onion, finely chopped	4 oz		¼ tsp	cayenne pepper	¼ tsp
4 tbsp	chopped parsley or fresh coriander	4 tbsp		15 cl	plain low-fat yogurt	¼ pint
3	garlic cloves, finely chopped	3		2 tbsp	red wine vinegar	2 tbsp
2 tbsp	grainy mustard	2 tbsp		1 tsp	prepared horseradish	1 tsp

Preheat the oven to 200°C (400°F or Mark 6). With a large knife, finely chop the fish. Put the fish in a large mixing bowl. Add 45 g (1½ oz) of the breadcrumbs, the egg, egg white, onion, all but 1 tablespoon of the parsley or coriander, the garlic, 1 tablespoon of the mustard, the liqueur if you are using it, the lemon juice, capers, paprika and cayenne pepper, and mix thoroughly.

Put the remaining breadcrumbs in a shallow bowl. Divide the fish mixture into eight equal portions. Pat one of the portions into a cake about 2 cm (¾ inch) thick. Coat the cake well

with breadcrumbs and place it on an oiled baking sheet. Repeat these steps to form the remaining portions into crumbed fishcakes. Bake the fishcakes for 20 minutes.

While the fishcakes are in the oven, prepare the sauce in a small bowl, mix the remaining mustard and the remaining parsley or coriander with the yogurt, the vinegar and the horseradish.

Serve the fishcakes with a dollop of sauce on the side.

Suggested accompaniment: red cabbage salad.

Baked Cod Plaki

Serves 6		Calories 150
Working time: about 30 minutes		Protein 17g
		Cholesterol 50mg
Total time: about 45 minutes		Total fat 5g
		Saturated fat 3g
		Sodium 350mg

500 g	cod fillets (or haddock, halibut or coley)	1 lb	3 tbsp	dry white wine	3 tbsp
2	large ripe tomatoes, sliced	2	60 g	crumbled feta cheese	2 oz
2	small onions, sliced	2	2 tbsp	chopped fresh parsley	2 tbsp
1	fennel bulb, cored, sliced crosswise, feathery tops reserved	1	4	oil-cured black olives, stoned and sliced	4
2	garlic cloves, finely chopped	2		freshly ground black pepper	
1 tbsp	chopped fresh oregano, or 2 tsp dried oregano	1 tbsp			

Preheat the oven to 190°C (375°F or Mark 5). Lightly oil a large baking dish; layer the tomatoes, onions, fennel, garlic and oregano in the bottom. Rinse the fish under cold running water and pat it dry with paper towels. Slice the fish crosswise into pieces about 5 cm (2 inches) wide. Arrange the fish on top of the vegetables and sprinkle it with the wine.

Cover the dish with the foil and bake the fish until it is opaque and feels firm to the touch – 15 to 20 minutes. Remove the dish from the oven. Sprinkle the fish with the crumbled feta cheese, parsley, black olives and some pepper. Garnish with some of the reserved fennel tops and serve immediately, spooning the pan juices over each portion.

Suggested accompaniment: steamed rice.

Baked Coley, Tomatoes, Courgettes and Provolone

Serves 4

Working time: about 15 minutes

Total time: about 30 minutes

Calories 215
Protein 27g
Cholesterol 90mg
Total fat 9g
Saturated fat 3g
Sodium 360mg

500 g	coley fillets (or cod or haddock)	1 lb	750 g	ripe tomatoes, skinned, seeded	1½ lb
¼ tsp	salt	¼ tsp		and chopped, or 400 g (14 oz)	
	freshly ground black pepper			canned whole tomatoes, drained,	
1 tbsp	virgin olive oil	1 tbsp		chopped and drained again	
2 tbsp	chopped fresh basil, or 1 tbsp	2 tbsp	1	small courgette, sliced diagonally	1
	dried basil			into thin ovals	
2	garlic cloves, finely chopped	2	60 g	provolone cheese, cut into thin,	2 oz
				narrow strips	

Preheat the oven to 200°C (400°F or Mark 6). Rinse the fillets under cold running water and pat them dry with paper towels. Sprinkle ⅛ teaspoon of the salt and some pepper over both sides of the fillets. Spread the oil in the bottom of an ovenproof casserole. Arrange the fillets in the casserole in a single layer.

Strew the basil and garlic over the fish, then cover the fish with the tomatoes. Arrange the courgette slices in a fish-scale pattern down the centre of the dish; sprinkle the remaining salt over them. Cover the dish with a piece of oiled greaseproof paper and bake it for 10 minutes. Remove the greaseproof paper and place the strips of provolone in a diamond pattern around the courgette. Cover the dish again and bake it until the fish feels firm to the touch – 3 to 5 minutes more. Serve immediately.

Hake and Four Peppers

Serves 6

Working (and total) time: about 30 minutes

Calories 210
Protein 23g
Cholesterol 60mg
Total fat 6g
Saturated fat 1g
Sodium 275mg

750 g	skinned hake fillet	**1¾ lb**	**2–3**	fresh hot green chili peppers, seeded and chopped	**2–3**
1 tsp	chili pepper	**1 tsp**	**2**	onions, chopped	**2**
⅛ tsp	cayenne pepper	**⅛ tsp**	**3**	garlic cloves, finely chopped	**3**
2 tsp	dried thyme	**2 tsp**	**2**	bay leaves	**2**
2 tbsp	virgin olive oil	**2 tbsp**	**35 cl**	dry white wine	**12 fl oz**
½ tsp	salt	**½ tsp**	**1**	sweet red pepper, seeded, deribbed and diced	**1**
3	sweet green peppers, seeded and deribbed, 1 coarsely chopped, the remaining 2 diced	**3**			

Preheat the oven to 180°C (350°F or Mark 4).

Combine the chili powder, cayenne pepper and 1 tsp of the thyme. Rinse fish and pat dry. Slice into six equal pieces; sprinkle on the spice mixture.

Heat the oil in a frying pan over medium-high heat. Add the fish pieces and cook them on one side for 3 mins. Turn them over and sprinkle with ¼ tsp of salt. Cook on the second side for 2 mins. Transfer to an ovenproof dish and bake for 5 mins.

Meanwhile, add the diced green peppers, the green chilies, onions, garlic, bay leaves and the remaining thyme to the pan. Cook, stirring, for 5 mins. Stir in the wine, red pepper and remaining salt.

Remove the fish from the oven and pour into the pan any juices from the dish. Return the fish to the oven for 5 mins. Increase the heat and cook the peppers until most of the liquid has evaporated – 5 mins. Remove the bay leaves.

While the peppers and fish are cooking, purée the chopped green pepper. Stir into the pepper mixture in the pan and cook it for 1 min more.

Remove the fish from the oven and spoon about half of the vegetables round it. Pass the remaining vegetables in a bowl.

Curried Grouper

Serves 4

Working
time: about
15 minutes

Total time:
about
25 minutes

Calories
260
Protein
25g
Cholesterol
40mg
Total fat
8g
Saturated fat
1g
Sodium
230mg

500 g	grouper fillet (or monkfish)	1 lb	125 g	chopped onion	4 oz
1 tbsp	curry powder	1 tbsp	1 tsp	fennel seeds, cracked	1 tsp
2 tbsp	safflower oil	2 tbsp	¼ tsp	salt	¼ tsp
3 tbsp	fresh lime juice	3 tbsp	150 g	shelled peas, blanched in	5 oz
	freshly ground black pepper			boiling water for 1 minute	
1	large red apple, cored and cut	1		dry white wine	
	into pieces				

Rinse the fillet under cold running water and pat it dry with paper towels. Cut the fillet into 2.5 cm (1 inch) pieces.

In a small bowl, combine the curry powder, 1 tablespoon of the oil, the lime juice and some pepper. Put the fish pieces, apple, onion and fennel seeds into a large bowl. Pour the curry mixture over the fish and mix well. Let the fish marinate for 10 minutes.

Pour the remaining oil into a large, heavy frying pan over high heat. When the oil is hot, add the contents of the bowl. Sprinkle in the salt and cook the curry for 3 minutes, stirring constantly. Add the peas and white wine and continue cooking the curry, stirring often, until the fish is firm to the touch – 2 to 3 minutes more. Transfer the curry to warmed serving dish.

Suggested accompaniments: mango chutney; diced cucumbers; unsalted peanuts; steamed rice.

Grouper with Shiitake Mushroom Sauce

Serves 4

Working
(and total)
time: about
35 minutes

Calories
210

Protein
23g

Cholesterol
40mg

Total fat
8g

Saturated fat
1g

Sodium
400mg

500 g	whole grouper fillet (or haddock or monkfish)	**1 lb**
15 g	dried shiitake or other Oriental mushrooms, soaked in 17.5 cl (6 fl oz) very hot water for 20 minutes	**½ oz**
4 tbsp	dry sherry	**4 tbsp**
2 tbsp	low-sodium soy sauce or shoyu	**2 tbsp**
2 tbsp	fresh lime juice	**2 tbsp**

1 tsp	sugar	**1 tsp**
1½ tsp	cornflour	**1½ tsp**
2 tbsp	safflower oil	**2 tbsp**
2	spring onions, trimmed and thinly sliced	**2**
1 tbsp	julienned fresh ginger root	**1 tbsp**
2	garlic cloves, thinly sliced	**2**
½ tsp	salt	**½ tsp**

Remove the mushrooms from their soaking liquid and slice them into thin pieces. Set aside. Pour 4 tablespoons of the soaking liquid into a mixing bowl, being careful to leave any grit behind. Stir in the sherry, soy sauce, 1 tablespoon of the lime juice and the sugar. Set aside.

Rinse the fillet under cold running water and pat it dry. Rub the fillet with the remaining lime juice, then rub the cornflour evenly over both sides of the fish.

Heat the oil in a large, heavy frying pan (preferably non-stick) over high heat. When the oil is hot, add the fish and sear it on one side for

2 minutes. Carefully turn the fillet over and sear it on the second side for 2 minutes. Transfer the fish to a plate.

Add the mushrooms, spring onions, ginger, garlic and pepper to the hot pan. Cook the mixture on high for 1 minute, then reduce the heat to low. Pour in the sherry mixture, replace the fillet, and cover the pan. Steam the fish until it is opaque – about 5 minutes. Transfer the fish to a warmed serving platter and spoon the sauce around it.

Suggested accompaniment: stir-fried red cabbage.

42

Stuffed Herrings

Serves 4

Working time: about 45 minutes

Total time: about 1 hour and 25 minutes

Calories 530

Protein 36g

Cholesterol 130mg

Total fat 40g

Saturated fat 9g

Sodium 350mg

4	herrings (350 g/12 oz each), dressed	4
15 g	unsalted butter	½ oz
1	onion, finely chopped	1
175 g	mushrooms, chopped	6 oz
1	lemon, rind only, finely grated	1
1 tbsp	lemon juice	1 tbsp
1 tbsp	chopped parsley	1 tbsp
1 tsp	fresh thyme leaves	1 tsp

60 g	fresh white breadcrumbs	2 oz
¼ tsp	salt	¼ tsp
	freshly ground black pepper	

Garnish
sliced mushrooms
parsley
lemon wedges

Preheat the oven to 200°C (400°F or Mark 6).

Wash the herrings thoroughly then pat them dry with paper towels. To remove the bones, take one fish at a time and place it on a work surface belly down. Gently but firmly press along the length of the backbone to flatten the fish. Turn the herring over, and run a thumb under the bones at each side of the backbone to loosen. Lift the bones out in one piece and snip the bone 2.5 cm (1 inch) from the tail.

Melt the butter in a heavy frying pan, add the onion and cook for 4 to 5 minutes until softened but not browned. Add the mushrooms and cook for 3 to 4 minutes until they are softened. Stir in the lemon rind and juice, parsley, thyme, and breadcrumbs. Season with the salt and pepper. Lay the herrings flat out, flesh side up. Spread some stuffing over each herring, then roll up from head to tail. Secure them by pressing the small piece of tail bone remaining into the flesh.

Place the herrings in a buttered ovenproof dish, cover with the foil and bake until the fish feels firm to the touch – about 35 minutes. Serve hot, garnished with mushrooms, parsley and lemon wedges.

Baked Herrings with Yogurt-Mint Sauce

Serves 4
Working time: about 15 minutes
Total time: about 1 hour

Calories	340
Protein	35g
Cholesterol	95mg
Total fat	18g
Saturated fat	5g
Sodium	200mg

4	herrings (or mackerel), about 250 g (8 oz) each, dressed	**4**
4 tbsp	chopped fresh mint	**4 tbsp**
4	garlic cloves, finely chopped	**4**
¼ tsp	ground cumin	**¼ tsp**
¼ tsp	cayenne pepper	**¼ tsp**
	Yogurt-Mint Sauce	
2 tbsp	chopped fresh mint	**2 tbsp**

¼ litre	plain low-fat yogurt	**8 fl oz**
1 tbsp	virgin olive oil	**1 tbsp**
3	garlic cloves, finely chopped	**3**
¼ tsp	ground cumin	**¼ tsp**
¼ tsp	ground coriander	**¼ tsp**
¼ tsp	ground turmeric	**¼ tsp**
¼ tsp	ground cardamom (optional)	**¼ tsp**
	mint sprigs for garnish	

Rinse the herrings under cold running water and pat them dry with paper towels.

In a small bowl, combine the 4 tablespoons of chopped mint, the garlic, cumin and cayenne pepper. Spread one quarter of this mixture inside the cavity of each herring. Cut shallow diagonal slashes at 2.5 cm (1 inch) intervals along the sides of each fish. Lay the fish on their sides in a lightly oiled baking dish. Let the herring marinate at room temperature for 30 minutes. Preheat the oven to 240°C (475°F or Mark 9).

While the fish is marinating, prepare the sauce. Stir the 2 tablespoons of chopped mint into the yogurt in a bowl, and set it aside. Heat the oil in a small heavy frying pan over medium-high heat, add the garlic and cook it until it is soft – about 2 minutes. Stir in the cumin, coriander, turmeric, and cardomom if you are using it, and cook the mixture for 30 seconds. Add the spice mixture to the minted yogurt and stir well.

Bake the fish until it feels firm to the touch and is opaque throughout – about 12 minutes. Serve it immediately, accompanied by the sauce and garnished with the mint sprigs.

Suggested accompaniment: steamed carrots.

Baked Grey Mullet

Serves 4

Working time: about 25 minutes

Total time: about 1 hour and 10 minutes

Calories 280
Protein 40g
Cholesterol 100mg
Total fat 10g
Saturated fat 4g
Sodium 230mg

1	grey mullet (1.5 to 2 kg/3 to 4 lb)	1
½ tsp	salt	½ tsp
	freshly ground black pepper	
1	large parsley sprig	1
1	large fresh thyme sprig	1
1	large fresh rosemary sprig	1
1	small lemon, cut into wedges	1

15 g	unsalted butter	½ oz
2	large onions, thinly sliced	2
3	garlic cloves, peeled and sliced	3
1 tbsp	virgin olive oil	1 tbsp
4 tbsp	dry white wine	4 tbsp
	lemon slices for garnish	

Preheat the oven to 200°C (400°F or Mark 6). Remove the fins, scales and viscera (but not the head) from the mullet. Wash the fish thoroughly under cold running water, then pat it dry with paper towels.

Season the inside of the mullet with a little of the salt and some pepper, and insert the parsley, thyme and rosemary sprigs and the lemon wedges.

Butter a large, shallow baking dish, then place the onion and garlic slices in the bottom of the dish. Set the mullet on top of the onion and garlic, and season with the remaining salt and

more pepper. Sprinkle the fish with the olive and white wine. Cover the dish with aluminium foil and bake the mullet in the oven until it is firm to the touch – 40 to 45 minutes. Serve hot, garnished with lemon slices.

Editor's Note: if you do not have a large baking dish, the mullet may be cooked wrapped in foil on a large baking sheet.

Suggested accompaniment: baked courgettes and tomatoes.

Grilled Mullet Coated with Cracked Black Pepper

Serves 6

Working time: about 35 minutes

Total time: about 4 hours and 30 minutes

Calories 150
Protein 21g
Cholesterol 85mg
Total fat 5g
Saturated fat 3g
Sodium 180mg

750 g	grey mullet fillets (or powan), skinned	**1½ lb**	**3 tbsp**	black peppercorns, cracked	**3 tbsp**
6 tbsp	fresh lemon juice	**6 tbsp**	**17.5 cl**	fish stock or vegetable stock	**6 fl oz**
12.5 cl	red wine vinegar	**4 fl oz**	**2 tsp**	fresh thyme, or ½ tsp dried thyme	**2 tsp**
3	garlic cloves, crushed	**3**	**30 g**	cold unsalted butter, cut into small pieces	**1 oz**
1½ tbsp	sugar	**1½ tbsp**	**2**	thyme sprigs for garnish	**2**
¼ tsp	salt	**¼ tsp**			

In a bowl just large enough to hold the fillets in one layer, mix the lemon juice, wine vinegar, garlic, sugar and salt. Lay fillets in the liquid, cover and marinate in the refrigerator for 4 hours; half way through, turn fillets over.

Preheat the grill or, if you are barbecuing, light the charcoal about 40 minutes before cooking time. Remove the fillets from the marinade and pat them dry with paper towels. Press half of the cracked pepper firmly into the flesh. Turn the fillets over and coat them with the remaining black pepper.

If you are grilling the fillets, cook them about 10 cm (4 inches) below the heat source for 4 to 5 minutes on each side.

If you are barbecuing the fillets, place them approximately 10 cm (4 inches) above the heat source and cook them on the first side for 6 minutes. Gently turn the fillets over and cook them on the second side until their flesh just flakes – about 6 minutes more.

While the fish is cooking, strain the marinade into a small non-reactive saucepan over medium heat and add the stock and thyme. Cook the mixture until it is reduced to about 12.5 cl (4 fl oz) – approximately 5 minutes. When the fillets are cooked, transfer them to a heated serving platter. Whisk the butter into the sauce, pour the sauce over the fillets, garnish with the thyme sprigs, and serve at once.

Spicy Grilled Shad

Serves 6

Working time: about 30 minutes

Total time: about 1 hour

Calories 250

Protein 20g

Cholesterol 90mg

Total fat 17g

Saturated fat 6g

Sodium 60mg

2	shad fillets, about 350 g (12 oz) each, (or rainbow trout or sea trout), unskinned	**2**
2 tbsp	dry vermouth	**2 tbsp**
1	lime, juice only	**1**
½	orange, juice only	**½**
1	fresh hot green chili pepper, seeded and finely chopped	**1**
1	garlic clove, finely chopped	**1**
1 tsp	fresh thyme, or ¼ tsp dried thyme	**1 tsp**
⅛ tsp	ground allspice	**⅛ tsp**
20 g	unsalted butter, cut into small cubes	**¾ oz**

In a small bowl, combine the vermouth, lime juice, orange juice, chili pepper, garlic, thyme and allspice. Set the bowl aside.

Rinse the fillets under cold running water and pat them dry with paper towels. To bone the fillets, place one of them skin side down on a work surface. With your fingers, locate the two rows of small bones; each row lies about about 2.5 cm (1 inch) on either side of the centre line of the fillet. Using a small, sharp knife, make a long cut on either side of one of the rows; take care not to penetrate the skin. Working from the head end towards the tail, gently pull the bones away in a single strip. Repeat the process to remove the other row of bones; bone the remaining fillet in the same manner.

Lay the fillets in an ovenproof dish and pour the marinade over them. Let the fillets marinate for 15 minutes. Preheat the grill.

Strain and reserve the marinade. Grill the fillets about 7.5 cm (3 inches) below the heat source, basting them every 3 minutes with the marinade, until their flesh is opaque – 10 to 12 minutes. Scatter the cubes of butter over the top; return the fillets to the grill and cook them a few seconds longer to melt the butter. Serve immediately.

Suggested accompaniment: salad of tropical fruits.

Skewered Sardines with Watercress Sauce

Serves 4

Working time: about 50 minutes

Total time: about 1 hour and 50 minutes

Calories 420

Protein 35g

Cholesterol 90mg

Total fat 25g

Saturated fat 7g

Sodium 230mg

8	sardines weighing 125 g (4 oz) each, or 1 kg (2 lb) small sardines	8
½ tsp	cayenne pepper	½ tsp
24	black peppercorns, crushed	24
1 tbsp	virgin olive oil	1 tbsp
½ tsp	salt	½ tsp
1	lime, rind only, finely grated watercress sprigs for garnish	1

	lemon wedges (optional)	
	Watercress Sauce	
30 cl	fish stock	½ pint
125 g	watercress, trimmed and washed	4 oz
15 g	unsalted butter	½ oz
15 g	flour	½ oz
1 tbsp	double cream	1 tbsp

Remove the fins, scales and viscera, but not the heads, from the sardines. Wash the fish under cold running water, then drain them dry on paper towels.

Put the cayenne pepper, peppercorns, oil, salt and grated lime rind in a large, shallow dish and mix them together. Place the sardines in the marinade, turning them until evenly coated. Cover and marinate for 1 hour.

To make the sauce, pour the fish stock into a small saucepan and bring to the boil. Add the watercress and cook gently for 10 minutes, until softened, then purée in a food processor or

blender for 1 minute.

Melt the butter in the pan, stir in the flour, then the puréed watercress. Bring to the boil, stirring all the time. Reduce the heat and simmer the sauce for 10 to 15 minutes.

Meanwhile, remove the sardines from the marinade and thread them on to wooden or metal skewers. Cook under a hot grill for 4 to 5 minutes, turning them once during cooking.

Stir the cream into the sauce then pour into a jug. Serve the sardines garnished with watercress and, if liked, lemon wedges. Hand the sauce separately.

Poached Turbot in Orange-Lemon Sauce

Serves 4

Working (and total) time: about 30 minutes

Calories 285
Protein 16g
Cholesterol 70mg
Total fat 18g
Saturated fat 6g
Sodium 230mg

500 g	turbot fillets (or flounder, halibut or sole)	**1 lb**
17.5 cl	fish stock	**6 fl oz**
17.5 cl	dry white wine	**6 fl oz**
15 cl	fresh orange juice	**¼ pint**
1 tbsp	fresh lemon juice	**1 tbsp**
2	shallots, finely chopped	**2**
1 tbsp	fresh thyme, or 1 tsp dried thyme	**1 tbsp**
	freshly ground black pepper	
30 g	unsalted butter	**1 oz**
1	large lettuce (about 150 g/5 oz), cored and washed	**1**
¼ tsp	salt	**¼ tsp**

Combine the fish stock, white wine, orange juice, half of the chopped shallots, half of the thyme and some black pepper in a large, non-reactive sauté pan. Bring to the boil, then reduce the heat to medium low. Simmer for 10 minutes.

Rinse the fillets under cold water and pat dry with paper towels. Slice each fillet diagonally in half to form one thick piece and one thin piece. Place the thicker fillets in the simmering liquid and poach gently for 1 minute. Add the thinner fillets and continue poaching fish until opaque and feels firm to the touch – 3 to 4 minutes. Transfer the fish to a plate and keep it warm.

Raise the heat to medium and simmer the liquid until it is reduced to 12.5 cl (4 fl oz). Strain through a sieve into a small pan and set it aside.

Melt 15 g (½ oz) of the butter in the same pan over medium heat. Add the remaining shallots and thyme, and cook them for 1 minute, stirring. Add the lettuce leaves, ⅛ teaspoon of the salt and some pepper. Cook the lettuce, stirring, until it has wilted – approximately 2 minutes. Place the lettuce on a warmed serving plate.

Reheat the sauce; stir in the remaining salt and whisk in the remaining butter. Put the fish pieces on the wilted lettuce, pour the sauce over the fish and serve immediately.

Suggested accompaniment: steamed courgettes with diced sweet red pepper.

Turbot Salad

Serves 4
as a starter

Working
time: about
30 minutes

Total time:
about
2 hours

Calories
220

Protein
30g

Cholesterol
95mg

Total fat
9g

Saturated fat
1g

Sodium
320mg

1 kg	turbot, cleaned	2 lb	½ tsp	salt	½ tsp
60 cl	court-bouillon	1 pint		freshly ground black pepper	
2 tbsp	virgin olive oil	2 tbsp	2 tbsp	chopped spring onions	2 tbsp
1	lemon, rind only, finely grated	1	2	kiwi fruit, peeled and sliced	2
2 tbsp	lemon juice	2 tbsp	350 g	tomatoes, sliced	12 oz
½ tsp	ground cardamom	½ tsp	1 tbsp	finely shredded basil leaves	1 tbsp
1 tbsp	chopped mixed herbs (parsley, marjoram and chives)	1 tbsp		watercress sprigs for garnish	

Rinse the turbot well under cold running water, removing any remaining viscera.

Pour the court-bouillon into a wide shallow saucepan. Place the turbot in the court-bouillon, cover the pan and cook for 10 minutes, or until the flesh flakes easily. Leave the turbot to cool in the court-bouillon – about 1½ hours.

Take the turbot out of the court-bouillon and skin it. Carefully remove the flesh from the bones, break the flesh into large flakes and set aside.

Place the olive oil, lemon rind, lemon juice, cardomom, mixed herbs, ¼ teaspoon of the salt and some pepper in a mixing bowl and blend well together. Add the spring onions, the flaked turbot and sliced kiwi fruit and mix gently.

Arrange the tomato slices neatly on a large serving plate or on individual plates. Season the tomatoes with the rest of the salt and some pepper, then sprinkle them with the basil. Spoon the turbot salad on to the tomatoes, garnish with the watercress sprigs and serve.

Editor's Note: The court-bouillon in which the turbot has been cooked makes an excellent fish stock. Strain and freeze it, or reserve it for later use.

Baked Powan with Garlic and Glazed Carrots

Serves 4

Working time: about 15 minutes

Total time: about 1 hour

Calories 265

Protein 23g

Cholesterol 55mg

Total fat 14g

Saturated fat 2g

Sodium 270mg

1	whole powan or hake (about 1 kg/ 2 lb), scaled and dressed	1
500 g	carrots, peeled and sliced diagonally into 2.5 cm (1 inch) pieces	1 lb
1 tbsp	fresh lemon juice	1 tbsp
	freshly ground black pepper	
6	garlic cloves, finely chopped	6
¼ tsp	salt	¼ tsp
1 tbsp	virgin olive oil	1 tbsp

Preheat the oven to 200°C (400°F or Mark 6). Put the carrots in a baking dish large enough to take the fish. Add the lemon juice, a generous grinding of pepper and a third of the chopped garlic. Pour 17.5 cl (6 fl oz) of water into the dish and toss the ingredients well.

Sprinkle the fish inside and out with the salt and some pepper, and rub the remaining garlic all over it. Push the carrots to the sides of the dish and lay the fish on the bottom. Dribble the oil over the fish. Bake, stirring the carrots every 15 minutes, until the fish is golden and the carrots are tender – about 45 minutes.

Suggested accompaniment: Brussels sprouts.

Carp in Red Wine

Serves 6

Working time: about 40 minutes

Total time: about 1 hour and 40 minutes

Calories 335
Protein 18g
Cholesterol 70mg
Total fat 13g
Saturated fat 3g
Sodium 160mg

1	whole carp or salmon (about 2 kg/	1
1	4½ lb), dressed and cut into 2.5 cm	1
	(1 inch) thick steaks	
250 g	pearl onions	8 oz
¾ litre	red wine	1¼ pints
¾ litre	fish stock	1¼ pints
3	whole cloves	3
1	small cinnamon stick	1
12	black peppercorns	12
¼ tsp	salt	¼ tsp
1	bay leaf	1
1 tbsp	safflower oil	1 tbsp
250 g	mushrooms, thickly sliced	8 oz
1 tsp	sugar	1 tsp
4 tbsp	sultanas	4 tbsp
15 g	cold unsalted butter, cut into	½ oz
	small pieces	
6	chervil or parsley sprigs	6

Cut off root ends of onions. Put in a bowl, cover with boiling water. When water has cooled, remove onions and squeeze out of their skins. Set aside.

In a sauté pan, combine wine, stock, cloves, cinnamon, peppercorns, salt and bay leaf. Bring to boil, reduce heat and simmer for 10 minutes.

Rinse steaks. Lay in the pan and poach, uncovered, until flesh is opaque and firm – 10 minutes. Remove steaks; cover and keep warm.

Return the poaching liquid to the boil and cook until reduced to ½ litre (16 fl oz).

Heat oil in another pan over meduim-high. Add mushrooms and sauté until tender and

golden. Transfer to a bowl, set aside. Add onions, sugar and ¼ litre (8 fl oz) of water to the pan. Cook until water has evaporated and onions are coated with a golden glaze – about 7 minutes. Transfer onions to the bowl with the mushrooms.

Strain the reduced stock into the pan. Add the sultanas and bring to boil. Simmer, scraping and stirring to dissolve the caramelized juices, until is reduced to about ¼ litre (8 fl oz) – about 5 minutes.

Reduce the heat to low and whisk in the butter. Add the reserved mushrooms and onions and reheat, pour the sauce over the steaks. Garnish with sprigs of chervil, serve immediately.

Carp with Paprika and Dill Cucumber Sauce

Serves 4

Working time: about 40 minutes

Total time: about 1 hour and 30 minutes

Calories 400
Protein 45g
Cholesterol 170mg
Total fat 22g
Saturated fat 6g
Sodium 265mg

1	carp (about 1.5 kg/3 lb)	1
½ tsp	salt	½ tsp
	freshly ground black pepper	
1 tbsp	lemon juice	1 tbsp
1	small bunch fresh dill	1
1	small bunch fresh parsley	1
15 g	butter	½ oz
1 tbsp	olive oil	1 tbsp
1	large onion, finely chopped	1
1	garlic clove, crushed	1

1 tbsp	paprika	1 tbsp
12.5 cl	fish stock	4 fl oz
15 g	flour	½ oz
12.5 cl	soured cream	4 fl oz
2	large pickled dill cucumbers, chopped	2

Garnish
lemon slices
sliced pickled dill cucumber
chopped parsley and dill

Preheat the oven to 200°C (400°F or Mark 6).

Remove the fins, scales and viscera (but not the head from the carp). Wash thoroughly under cold running water then pat dry.

Season the inside of the carp with half the salt, some pepper and the lemon juice. Place the dill and parsley inside the carp then set aside.

Heat the butter and oil in a frying pan, add onion and cook over low heat for 5 to 6 mins until the onion is softened but not browned. Stir the garlic and paprika into the onion, pour in 4 tablespoons of fish stock and bring to the boil.

Pour the mixture into a shallow dish and place

the carp on top. Cover with foil, cook in the oven until firm to the touch – 45 to 50 mins.

Lift the carp from the dish on to a hot serving dish. Cover, keep warm while making sauce.

Transfer onion and cooking juices to a saucepan, then stir in the flour and the remaining fish stock. Bring to the boil, stirring. Stir in the soured cream, pickled cucumbers and remaining salt. Reduce the heat and simmer for 3 to 4 minutes. Pour into a hot serving bowl or jug.

Garnish with lemon, cucumber and dill. Serve immediately, accompanied by the sauce.

Spiced Carp with Almonds and Raisins

Serves 4

Working time: about 25 minutes

Total time: about 50 minutes

Calories 300

Protein 25g

Cholesterol 170mg

Total fat 17g

Saturated fat 7g

Sodium 275mg

1.5 kg	carp, dressed and cut into steaks, about 4 cm (1½ inches) thick	3 lb
½ tsp	salt	½ tsp
	freshly ground black pepper	
½ tbsp	olive oil	½ tbsp
60 g	almonds, blanched and halved	2 oz
15 g	unsalted butter	½ oz
60 g	raisins	2 oz

¼ tsp	ground cumin	¼ tsp
¼ tsp	ground allspice	¼ tsp
¼ tsp	ground mace	¼ tsp
¼ tsp	ground cinnamon	¼ tsp
Garnish		
	orange wedges	
	parsley	

Preheat the oven to 200°C (400°F or Mark 6).

Lay a piece of aluminium foil on a baking sheet, place the carp steaks side by side on the foil and season with the salt and some pepper.

Heat the oil in a heavy frying pan, add the almonds and fry them gently until lightly browned. Add the butter to the pan and stir in the raisins and spices. Heat for 1 minute, then pour over the carp steaks. Fold the foil to enclose the carp completely and bake in the oven for 25 to 30 minutes, until the flesh is opaque and feels firm to the touch.

Arrange the steaks on a hot serving dish and garnish with orange wedges and parsley. Serve immediately.

Salmon-Stuffed Tuna in Lettuce Leaves

Serves 6

**Working
time: about
30 minutes**

**Total time:
about
40 minutes**

**Calories
255**

**Protein
35g**

**Cholesterol
50mg**

**Total fat
10g**

**Saturated fat
2g**

**Sodium
165mg**

1 kg	fresh tuna (or swordfish), trimmed and cut into 6 small steaks	**2 lb**
12	large round lettuce leaves (or spinach leaves)	**12**
2	paper-thin slices smoked salmon, each slice cut into three strips freshly ground black pepper	**2**

1	shallot, finely chopped	**1**
55 cl	fish stock	**18 fl oz**
3	sticks celery, julienned	**3**
2	carrots, peeled and julienned	**2**
1	large leek, trimmed, washed thoroughly to remove all grit, and julienned	**1**

Blanch the lettuce leaves in a large pan of boiling water for 10 seconds. Refresh them under cold running water. Carefully spread out the leaves – they tear easily – on a cloth. Preheat the oven to 200°C (400°F or Mark 6).

Lightly oil a baking dish large enough to hold the fish steaks in a single layer. With a sharp knife, cut a pocket in the side of each steak. Insert a salmon strip in each pocket, sprinkle the steaks with some pepper, and wrap each in two lettuce leaves. Set the wrapped steaks in the baking dish. Scatter the shallot over the steaks. Bring the stock to the boil and pour ½ litre (16 fl oz) of it over the fish. Cover the dish with aluminium foil, its shiny side down.

Put in the oven; immediately reduce heat to 180°C (350°F or Mark 4), and bake for 15 minutes.

About 5 minutes before the fish finishes baking, put the celery, carrots and leek in a saucepan. Pour in the remaining stock and turn the heat to medium high. Cover the pan and steam the vegetables until they are tender – 3 to 5 minutes.

Remove from the oven; spoon a little of the fish-cooking liquid into the saucepan with the vegetables, transfer the vegetables to a warmed serving platter. Carefully transfer the fish to the platter with a fish slice and serve immediately.

Suggested accompaniment: crusty bread.

Marinated Fresh Tuna with Peppers

Serves 6 as a first course		Calories 145	
Working time: about 30 minutes		Protein 15g	
Total time: about 2 hours and 30 minutes		Cholesterol 25mg	
		Total fat 9g	
		Saturated fat 2g	
		Sodium 75mg	

350 g	fresh tuna	**12 oz**	**⅛ tsp**	salt	**⅛ tsp**
2 tbsp	finely chopped red onion	**2 tbsp**		freshly ground black pepper	
4 tbsp	coarsely chopped fresh basil	**4 tbsp**	**1**	sweet red pepper	**1**
2 tbsp	virgin olive oil	**2 tbsp**	**1**	sweet green pepper	**1**
1 tbsp	fresh lemon juice	**1 tbsp**	**1**	sweet yellow pepper	**1**

Rinse the tuna under cold running water and pat it dry with paper towels. Trim off and discard any dark red meat from the tuna. Cut the tuna into slices about 9 mm (⅜ inch) thick. If any slice is too thick, pound it with the heel of your hand to flatten it. Cut the slices into strips about 1 cm (½ inch) wide and 5 cm (2 inches) long.

Place the tuna strips in a shallow dish with the onion and chopped basil. In a small bowl, whisk together the oil, lemon juice, salt and pepper; pour this mixture over the pepper. With a rubber spatula, toss the tuna very gently until the strips are thoroughly coated. Cover the dish and refrigerate it for 2 hours, turning the tuna strips occasionally.

Preheat the grill. Grill the peppers about 7.5 cm (3 inches) below the heat source, turning them with tongs as they blister, until their skins are blackened all over – approximately 15 minutes. Put the peppers in a large bowl and cover it tightly with plastic film (the trapped steam will loosen their skins). When the peppers are cool enough to handle, peel, seed and derib them. Quarter each pepper lengthwise.

To serve, arrange the marinated tuna strips and the roasted peppers on a platter.

Suggested accompaniment: French bread.

Editor's Note: Because the tuna in this recipe is not cooked, only the freshest possible fish should be used.

Grilled Tuna with White Beans and Red Onions

Serves 6

Working time: about 20 minutes

Total time: about 1 day

Calories 330

Protein 27g

Cholesterol 30mg

Total fat 13g

Saturated fat 2g

Sodium 230mg

500 g	fresh tuna (or swordfish)	**1 lb**
180 g	dried white haricot beans, soaked for at least 8 hours in water	**6 oz**
2	garlic cloves	**2**
1	strip of lemon rind	**1**
½ tsp	salt	**½ tsp**
2	large red onions, thinly sliced	**2**
12.5 cl	red wine vinegar	**4 fl oz**

1 tsp	brown sugar	**1 tsp**
2	lemons, juice only	**2**
3 tbsp	virgin olive oil	**3 tbsp**
1½ tsp	fresh thyme, or ½ tsp dried thyme	**1½ tsp**
	freshly ground black pepper	
1 tsp	fresh rosemary, or ¼ tsp dried rosemary	**1 tsp**
	basil leaves for garnish	

Drain the beans and put in a pan with the garlic and lemon rind. Pour in water to cover by about 2.5 cm (1 inch). Boil for 10 minutes, reduce heat and cook for 30 minutes. Stir in ¼ teaspoon of the salt and continue cooking until beans are tender – 15 to 30 minutes more.

Put the onions, vinegar and sugar in a small saucepan over medium-low. Simmer, stirring often, for 10 minutes. Transfer to a small bowl and let them cool slightly, then refrigerate them.

In a bowl, whisk together lemon juice, 2 tablespoons of the oil, remaining salt, half of the thyme and a generous grinding of pepper. When beans are tender, drain, discard rind and garlic cloves. Add beans to bowl and stir well.

Preheat grill. Rinse tuna under cold water and pat dry with paper towels. Trim any very dark red meat from the tuna. Cut into 2.5 cm (1 inch) cubes and put in a baking dish. Add remaining oil, remaining thyme, rosemary and some pepper, toss well to coat the tuna. Grill the tuna on the first side for 2 minutes. Turn the pieces over and grill, without overcooking, until they are opaque – 1 to 2 minutes more.

Transfer beans to a serving dish; arrange tuna cubes on top of beans and onions alongside. Garnish with basil and serve warm or cold.

Suggested accompaniment: steamed artichoke.

Grilled Eel in Ginger-Sherry Sauce on Rice Fingers

Serves 4
as a first
course

Working
time: about
30 minutes

Total time:
about
40 minutes

Calories
420

Protein
20g

Cholesterol
95mg

Total fat
14g

Saturated fat
3g

Sodium
370mg

500 g	eel	**1 lb**	
1 tsp	rice vinegar	**1 tsp**	
200 g	glutinous rice, preferably sushi rice	**7 oz**	
1 tsp	wasabi (Japanese horseradish powder), mixed with enough water to form a paste	**1 tsp**	

Ginger-Sherry Sauce		
4 tbsp	dry sherry	**4 tbsp**
2 tbsp	low-sodium soy sauce or shoyu	**2 tbsp**
1 tbsp	finely chopped fresh ginger root	**1 tbsp**
1 tbsp	sugar	**1 tbsp**
1 tbsp	honey	**1 tbsp**
⅛ tsp	cayenne pepper	**⅛ tsp**

Boil ½ litre (16 fl oz) of water and the vinegar. Add rice, cover and reduce heat. Cook rice, stirring occasionally, until the liquid has been absorbed – 20 minutes. Set aside.

While rice is cooking, fillet the eel. Place it on its belly. Cut head off and discard. Holding a knife parallel to the eel, cut along one side of dorsal fin, following the contour of the backbone until the fillet is freed. Repeat on the other side. Cut away any viscera. Rinse fillets and cut in half diagonally.

Pour 1 cm (½ inch) water into a pan. Put a bamboo steamer basket in the water. (Alternatively, put a heatproof cup in the pan and lay a heatproof plate on top.) Place the fillets in the steamer basket or plate, bring to the boil.

Reduce heat to low, cover and steam for 7 mins.

While the fillets are steaming, mix sherry, soy sauce, ginger, sugar, honey and cayenne pepper in a small saucepan. Bring to the boil, then reduce the heat to low. Simmer to thicken and reduce by half – 7 to 10 mins. Preheat the grill.

Brush sauce on both sides of the fillets and let them stand for 5 minutes. Brush on more sauce and grill until they are crisp – 2 to 4 mins. Turn the fillets over, brush on more sauce and grill them until crisp – 2 to 3 mins.

Form the cooled rice into 16 'fingers', and arrange on a platter. Slice eel into 16 pieces and place each on a rice finger. Brush with remaining sauce and serve with wasabi.

Eel with Spinach and Leeks

Serves 6

Working
time: about
20 minutes

Total time:
about
40 minutes

Calories
370

Protein
25g

Cholesterol
125mg

Total fat
21g

Saturated fat
4g

Sodium
130mg

1 kg	eel, skinned, cleaned and cut into 5 cm (2 inch) pieces	**2 lb**
1 tbsp	safflower oil	**1 tbsp**
500 g	leeks, trimmed, split, washed thoroughly to remove any grit, and sliced	**1 lb**
2	garlic cloves, finely chopped	**2**

1½ tsp	fresh thyme, or ½ tsp dried thyme	**1½ tsp**
2 tbsp	chopped fresh mint	**2 tbsp**
¼ litre	dry white wine	**8 fl oz**
½ litre	fish or unsalted chicken stock	**16 fl oz**
1 kg	spinach, washed, stemmed and coarsely chopped	**2 lb**
2 tbsp	chopped fresh parsley	**2 tbsp**

Heat the oil in a large, heavy frying pan over medium heat. Add the leeks, garlic, thyme and 1 tablespoon of the mint. Sauté the mixture for 2 minutes. Pour in the wine, cover the pan, and reduce the heat to medium low; cook the mixture until the leeks are tender – about 10 minutes.

Pour the stock into the pan and bring the liquid to the boil. Add the eel, reduce the heat to maintain a simmer, and cover the pan. Cook until the eel is opaque and feels firm to the touch – about 10 minutes.

About 5 minutes before the eel is done, put the spinach, with only the water that clings to it

from washing, in a deep pan. Set the pan over medium-high heat, cover it tightly, and steam the spinach until it is wilted – about 3 minutes. With a slotted spoon, transfer the spinach to a heated serving dish. Arrange the eel pieces on top of the spinach.

Add the remaining mint and the parsley to the eel-cooking liquid. Boil the liquid until it is reduced to ½ litre (16 fl oz) – about 3 minutes. Pour the sauce over the eel and serve immediately.

Suggested accompaniment: steamed potatoes or rice.

Sautéed Mackerel with Toasted Hazelnuts

Serves 4

Working (and total) time: about 35 minutes

Calories 440

Protein 26g

Cholesterol 120mg

Total fat 34g

Saturated fat 9g

Sodium 320mg

500 g	large mackerel fillets	**1 lb**
45 g	shelled hazelnuts	**1½ oz**
2 tbsp	plain flour	**2 tbsp**
1 tbsp	safflower oil	**1 tbsp**
¼ tsp	salt	**¼ tsp**
	freshly ground black pepper	
15 g	unsalted butter	**½ oz**
2	spring onions, thinly sliced	**2**

2	garlic cloves, finely chopped	**2**
4 tbsp	balsamic vinegar, or 3 tbsp red wine vinegar mixed with 1 tsp honey	**4 tbsp**
1 tbsp	fresh lime or lemon juice	**1 tbsp**
1	tomato, cored, cut into thin strips	**1**
4 tbsp	chopped fresh basil or flat-leaf parsley	**4 tbsp**

Preheat the oven to 180°C (350°F or Mark 4). Spread the hazelnuts in a single layer in a baking tin and toast them in the oven for 10 minutes. Rub the hazelnuts with a tea towel to remove most of their papery skin. Coarsely chop the nuts and set them aside.

Rinse the fillets under cold running water and pat them dry with paper towels. Cut the fillets into a total of four serving pieces and dust them with flour; pat off any excess. Heat the oil in a large, heavy frying pan over medium-high heat. Add the fillets and sauté them on one side for 4 minutes. Turn them over and sprinkle them with the salt and some pepper. Cook the fish on

the second side until it feels firm to the touch – 3 to 4 minutes. Transfer the fillets to a serving platter and keep them warm.

Melt the butter in the frying pan. Add the hazelnuts and sauté them for 2 minutes. Stir in the spring onions, garlic, vinegar and citrus juice. Cook the mixture for 1 minute, stirring all the while. Add the tomato, the basil or parsley, and some pepper. Cook the mixture for 1 minute more, stirring constantly, then spread it evenly over the fish. Serve immediately.

Suggested accompaniment: baked sweet potatoes.

Salmon with Fresh Basil Sauce

Serves 4

Working time: about 15 minutes

Total time: about 30 minutes

Calories
285
Protein
24g
Cholesterol
60mg
Total fat
18g
Saturated fat
6g
Sodium
190mg

500 g	salmon fillets, skinned	**1 lb**	**2**	shallots, thinly sliced	**2**
1 tbsp	safflower oil	**1 tbsp**	**1**	garlic clove, finely chopped	**1**
¼ tsp	salt	**¼ tsp**	**125 g**	basil leaves	**4 oz**
	freshly ground black pepper		**4 tbsp**	fish stock or dry white wine	**4 tbsp**
1½ tbsp	fresh lemon juice	**1½ tbsp**	**4 tbsp**	double cream	**4 tbsp**

Rinse the fillets under cold running water and pat them dry with paper towels. Cut the fish diagonally across the grain into slices about 2.5 cm (1 inch) thick.

Pour the oil into a large, heavy frying pan over high heat. When the oil is hot, add the fish pieces and cook them on the first side for 3 minutes. Carefully turn the pieces over and sprinkle them with ⅛ teaspoon of the salt, a generous grinding of pepper and the lemon juice. Cook them on the second side until they are barely done – about 3 minutes more. Remove the pan from the heat.

Transfer the fish to a warmed serving platter and cover the platter with aluminium foil. Return the pan to the stove over medium heat. Add the shallots and garlic and cook them, stirring constantly, for 30 seconds. Add the basil and the stock or wine, and simmer the mixture for 1 minute. Stir in the cream, the remaining salt and some more pepper, and continue simmering the sauce until it thickens slightly – about 2 minutes. Pour the sauce over the fish and serve immediately.

Suggested accompaniment: grilled sweet red peppers.

Pickled Salmon with Red Potatoes

Serves 6 as a first course

Working time: about 25 minutes

Total time: 24 hours

Calories 250
Protein 24g
Cholesterol 40mg
Total fat 11g
Saturated fat 2g
Sodium 115mg

750 g	fresh salmon fillets, skinned	**1¼ lb**
30 g	fresh dill sprigs	**1 oz**
2 tbsp	virgin olive oil	**2 tbsp**
30 cl	red wine vinegar or white wine vinegar	**½ pint**
1	bunch spring onions, trimmed and sliced diagonally into 1 cm (½ inch) pieces	**1**
1	lemon, juice only	**1**
1	orange, juice only	**1**
1 tbsp	mustard seeds	**1 tbsp**
1 tsp	black peppercorns, cracked	**1 tsp**
3	bay leaves	**3**
½ tsp	salt	**½ tsp**
1 tsp	whole cloves	**1 tsp**
500 g	red potatoes, skins left on	**1 lb**

Rinse the fillets under cold running water and pat them dry with paper towels. Cut the fish into chunks about 2 cm (¾ inch) thick.

In a large glass bowl, combine the salmon chunks, three quarters of the dill sprigs and the oil. Put the vinegar, lemon juice, orange juice, spring onions, mustard seeds, peppercorns, bay leaves, salt and cloves in a large, non-reactive saucepan. Bring the mixture to the boil, then pour it over the salmon chunks. Gently stir the marinade and salmon to coat the pieces. Allow the marinade to cool, then cover the bowl and refrigerate it for at least 24 hours.

At the end of the marinating time, strain 17.5 cl (6 fl oz) of the marinade into a second glass bowl. Add the remaining dill sprigs to the strained marinade. Cut the potatoes into 2.5 cm (1 inch) pieces and place them in a steamer. Fill a saucepan about 2.5 cm (1 inch) deep with water. Put the steamer in the saucepan, cover the pan and bring the water to a simmer. Steam the potatoes until they are soft – 10 to 15 minutes. Immediately transfer the potatoes to the strained marinade; stir gently to coat the potatoes.

Serve potatoes at once with the cold salmon.

Suggested accompaniment: dark rye or wholemeal bread.

Whole Poached Salmon

Serves 8

Working (and total) time: about 30 minutes

Calories 280
Protein 28g
Cholesterol 110mg
Total fat 17g
Saturated fat 4g
Sodium 90mg

| 1 | whole salmon (about 2 kg/ 4 lb), gutted | 1 |
| 4 litres | court-bouillon | 7 pints |

Garnish

125 g	spinach, washed, stemmed and thinly sliced	4 oz
250 g	daikon radish, peeled and julienned	8 oz
1	red plum, stoned and sliced	1

Pour the court-bouillon into a fish kettle or pan large enough to accommodate the salmon.

Wash the salmon inside and out under cold running water. Wrap the salmon in a double thickness of muslin that is about 25 cm (10 inches) longer than the fish. Knot each end of the muslin and secure it by tying string round the fish in two or three places.

Holding the knotted ends of the cloth, gently lower the fish into the court-bouillon. Bring the liquid to a simmer over medium heat. Cover the pan, reduce the heat to low, and cook the salmon for 8 minutes per 2.5 cm (1 inch) of thickness (measured at its thickest point).

Let the fish cool in the court-bouillon, then carefully transfer it to a work surface. Cut away

the strings, untie the knots, and unwrap the muslin, leaving the fish on the cloth. Cut out all but the pectoral fins of the fish. Make a long cut down the back and down the belly of the salmon. Cut through the skin at the base of the tail. Then, working from the base of the tail towards the head, gently pull off the skin in strips.

Carefully transfer the fish to a long platter, placing it skinned side down. Make another cut at the base of the tail and remove the skin from the second side.

Combine the sliced spinach and julienned radish and arrange them round the salmon. Garnish with the plum slices. Serve the salmon warm or cold.

Soufflé of Smoked Trout

1	small smoked trout fillet, skinned and boned, the flesh shredded (about 60 g/2 oz)	1
4	freshwater trout, filleted (about 500 g/1 lb of fillets) or 500 g (1 lb) sea trout fillets	4
2 tbsp	finely cut fresh dill	2 tbsp
2 tbsp	fresh lemon juice	2 tbsp
15 g	unsalted butter	½ oz
1	onion, finely chopped	1
6 tbsp	plain flour	6 tbsp

¼ litre	skimmed milk	8 fl oz
¼ litre	fish stock, or an additional ¼ litre (8 fl oz) skimmed milk	8 fl oz
¼ tsp	fresh thyme, or ⅛ tsp dried thyme	¼ tsp
⅛ tsp	grated nutmeg	⅛ tsp
¼ tsp	salt	¼ tsp
	freshly ground black pepper	
2	egg yolks	2
8	egg whites	8
⅛ tsp	cream of tartar	⅛ tsp

Preheat the oven to 220°C (425°F or Mark 7). Rinse the fillets and pat dry with paper towels. Wrap in foil, and set on a baking sheet. Bake until they are opaque – 15 minutes.

Unwrap and spread out to cool. Flake the flesh, picking out all the bones. In a bowl, combine fresh and smoked trout, dill and lemon juice. Set aside.

Melt the butter in a saucepan over medium-high. Add onion, cook it until translucent. Put flour in a bowl and stir in the milk and stock, if you are using it. Pour into the pan and bring to the boil, whisking.

Remove from the heat and whisk in thyme, nutmeg, salt, pepper and egg yolks; set aside and keep warm.

Mix the egg whites with the cream of tartar; beat into stiff peaks. Stir the milk-and-stock mixture into the fish mixture. Stir ¼ of the egg whites into fish mixture, fold in the remaining whites.

Pour the mixture into a lightly buttered 2 litre (3½ pint) soufflé dish. Put the dish in the oven. Reduce the temperature to 190°C (375°F or Mark 5). Bake until soufflé is puffed, golden and set – about 45 mins. Serve immediately.

Cucumber-Stuffed Trout with Dill Sauce

Serves 4

Working time: about 30 minutes

Total time: about 40 minutes

Calories 440
Protein 29g
Cholesterol 80mg
Total fat 23g
Saturated fat 4g
Sodium 430mg

4	rainbow trout, (about 250 g/8 oz) each (or redfish or Norway haddock), cleaned, scaled and filleted, the skin is left on	**4**
2½ tbsp	safflower oil	**2½ tbsp**
250 g	cucumber, peeled and thinly sliced	**8 oz**
1 tbsp	finely chopped shallot	**1 tbsp**
¼ tsp	salt	**¼ tsp**
	freshly ground black pepper	
4 tbsp	dry vermouth	**4 tbsp**
60 g	flour	**2 oz**
2	egg whites, lightly beaten	**2**
100 g	dry breadcrumbs	**3½ oz**
	dill sprigs for garnish	
	Dill Sauce	
75 g	finely cut fresh dill	**2½ oz**
¼ litre	plain low-fat yogurt	**8 fl oz**
1 tbsp	dried dill	**1 tbsp**
2 tbsp	finely chopped shallot	**2 tbsp**
⅛ tsp	salt	**⅛ tsp**
⅛ tsp	white pepper	**⅛ tsp**

Preheat the oven to 190°C (375°F or Mark 5).

Pour ½ tbsp of the oil into a shallow casserole over medium-high. Add cucumber, sauté until it begins to soften – about 2 mins. Add shallot, stir, until translucent. Reduce to low; season with ⅛ tsp of salt and some black pepper. Pour in vermouth and simmer until nearly all the liquid has evaporated – about 3 mins. Set aside.

Combine all sauce ingredients; set aside.

Lay one half of each fish skin side down. Season with black pepper and salt. Arrange cucumber slices on each half, reserving a few for garnish. Lay remaining fillets on top to form packets.

Holding each packet together, coat with flour, then egg white, then breadcrumbs. Wipe out the casserole, set it over medium heat and pour in the remaining oil. Fry the packets on one side until lightly browned – about 2 minutes. Turn over and transfer the casserole to the oven; bake the fish until easily flaked with a fork at the thickest point – 4 to 5 mins.

Transfer to a platter. Spoon some dill sauce over, serving rest on the side. Garnish with cucumber and dill.

Grilled Trout and Dried Figs

Serves 4		**Calories 435**
Working time: about 1 hour		**Protein 33g**
		Cholesterol 95mg
Total time: 1 hour and 10 minutes		**Total fat 11g**
		Saturated fat 2g
		Sodium 255mg

4	trout, about 350 g (12 oz) each, cleaned, the fins removed	**4**
12	dried figs, halved lengthwise	**12**
¼ litre	medium-dry sherry	**8 fl oz**
3 tbsp	balsamic vinegar or sherry vinegar	**3 tbsp**

1 tbsp	maple syrup or honey	**1 tbsp**
1 tbsp	Dijon mustard	**1 tbsp**
¼ tsp	salt	**¼ tsp**
	freshly ground black pepper	

Put the figs in a saucepan over low heat with the sherry and 2 tablespoons of the vinegar. Simmer the figs for 10 minutes. Remove the pan from the heat and let the figs steep in the liquid.

While the figs are steeping, butterfly the trout, as follows. Cut off and discard the heads of the trout. With a small, sharp knife, cut through the back of a trout on one side of its backbone from the head to within 2.5 cm (1 inch) of the tail. Repeat the cutting procedure on the other side of the backbone. Using kitchen scissors, sever the backbone near the tail; lift it out with your fingers. With tweezers, pull out any small bones remaining in the trout. Rinse the fish under cold water, then pat it dry with paper towels. Repeat these steps to butterfly the remaining trout.

Preheat the grill. Remove the figs from their steeping liquid and set them aside. Stir the maple syrup or honey into the liquid, then cook the liquid over medium heat until only about 6 tablespoons remains – approximately 5 minutes. Whisk the mustard and the remaining vinegar into the sauce. Remove from the heat.

Set the butterflied trout, skin side down, on a grill pan and tuck their sides under slightly. Sprinkle the fish with the salt and pepper and brush with about half of the sauce. Grill the trout until their flesh is opaque – about 5 minutes. Put the figs on the grill pan with the fish. Brush the fish and figs with the remaining sauce and grill them together for 1 minute before serving.

Suggested accompaniment: stir-fried carrots.

Poached Trout with Horseradish Sauce

Serves 4

Working time: about 45 minutes

Total time: about 3 hours and 45 minutes

Calories 265

Protein 42g

Cholesterol 90mg

Total fat 11g

Saturated fat 2g

Sodium 190mg

4	trout (250 to 350 g/8 to 12 oz each), gutted, fins removed	**4**
60 cl	court-bouillon	**1 pint**
	Horseradish Sauce	
1 tbsp	finely grated fresh horseradish, or 2 tsp prepared horseradish	**1 tbsp**
1 tbsp	lemon juice	**1 tbsp**
1 tsp	Dijon mustard	**1 tsp**
12.5 cl	soured cream	**4 fl oz**
	freshly ground black pepper	
	Garnish	
	thinly sliced radishes	
	fresh herbs (chervil, tarragon or chives)	
	lemon slices	
	finely shredded lettuce leaves	

Wash the trout thoroughly under cold running water then pat them dry with paper towels.

Pour the court-bouillon into a wide shallow saucepan and bring it to the boil. Place the trout in a single layer in the court-bouillon, ensuring that they are well covered. Cover the saucepan, reduce the heat to low and simmer for 10 minutes. Remove from the heat and allow the trout to cool in the court-bouillon until quite cold (overnight, if desired).

Meanwhile, make the sauce. Blend the horseradish with the remaining ingredients in a small bowl. Pour the sauce into a serving bowl, cover and refrigerate until ready to serve.

Lift the trout from the court-bouillon on to a large wire rack placed over a tray. Very carefully remove the skin from the top side of each fish. Garnish decoratively with radishes, fresh herbs and lemon slices.

Place the trout on a large serving dish, or individual plates, and surround them with finely shredded lettuce leaves. Serve with the horseradish sauce.

Suggested accompaniment: salad of sliced artichoke hearts and asparagus.

Mackerel Brochettes

Serves 4

Working time: about 45 minutes

Total time: 1 hour and 45 minutes

Calories 485

Protein 31g

Cholesterol 135mg

Total fat 20g

Saturated fat 4g

Sodium 220mg

500 g	mackerel fillets	**1 lb**
1	fennel bulb, base cut into 1 cm	**1**
	($\frac{1}{2}$ inch) squares, feathery tops reserved	
8	pearl onions	**8**
1	garlic clove	**1**
$\frac{1}{8}$ tsp	salt	**$\frac{1}{8}$ tsp**
1	lemon, juice only	**1**
12.5 cl	dry white wine	**4 fl oz**
1 tsp	fresh thyme, or $\frac{1}{2}$ tsp dried thyme	**1 tsp**
8	cherry tomatoes	**8**
1	courgette, thickly sliced	**1**
8	button mushrooms, wiped clean	**8**

250 g	fresh spinach fettuccine	**8 oz**
	Peppery Tomato Sauce	
1 tbsp	virgin olive oil	**1 tbsp**
2	shallots, finely chopped	**2**
2	garlic cloves, finely chopped	**2**
1.25 kg	ripe tomatoes, skinned, seeded	**2$\frac{1}{2}$ lb**
	and coarsely chopped	
1 tsp	fresh thyme, or $\frac{1}{2}$ tsp dried thyme	**1 tsp**
$\frac{1}{8}$ tsp	salt	**$\frac{1}{8}$ tsp**
$\frac{1}{8}$ tsp	cayenne pepper	**$\frac{1}{8}$ tsp**
	freshly ground black pepper	

Rinse fish, pat dry. Cut into thick chunks.

Boil the fennel squares for 3 mins. Remove from the water. Parboil the pearl onions for 3 mins; when cool, peel.

Pound together the garlic and salt to a paste. Stir in lemon juice, wine and thyme. Finely chop 1 tbsp of the feathery fennel and add to the marinade; reserve remainder for garnish. Add the fish, fennel, pearl onions, cherry tomatoes, courgette and mushrooms. Stir. Refrigerate for 1 hour, stirring from time to time.

To make the sauce, heat the oil in a frying pan over low heat. Cook shallots and garlic, until the shallots are soft. Stir in tomatoes, the thyme, seasoning. Cook for 15 mins; sieve and keep warm.

Preheat the grill or barbecue.

Thread fish and vegetables onto eight long skewers and grill, turning occasionally, until tender – 8 to 10 mins.

Cook fettuccine in boiling water until *al dente* – about 2 mins. Serve two brochettes per person, with fettuccine tossed in sauce and fennel top garnish.

Mackerel Fillets with Rhubarb Sauce

Serves 4

Working time: about 10 minutes

Total time: about 40 minutes

Calories 325

Protein 22g

Cholesterol 90mg

Total fat 16g

Saturated fat 3g

Sodium 175mg

500 g	mackerel fillets, skin left on	**1 lb**	
2 tbsp	sugar	**2 tbsp**	
1 tbsp	red wine vinegar	**1 tbsp**	
2	navel oranges, the julienned rind and juice of 1 reserved, the other peeled and sliced into thin rounds	**2**	

250 g	rhubarb, thinly sliced	**8 oz**	
⅛ tsp	ground cumin	**⅛ tsp**	
¼ tsp	salt	**¼ tsp**	
	freshly ground black pepper		
1 tbsp	safflower oil	**1 tbsp**	

In a small, heavy-bottomed saucepan over high heat, cook the sugar, stirring constantly with a wooden spoon, until it melts and forms a syrup. Cook, stirring, to a light caramel colour – 30 seconds to 1 minute. (If the sugar turns dark brown, discard it and start again.) Standing well back, immediately pour in the vinegar and orange juice; the sugar will harden. Reduce the heat to medium low and cook the mixture until it becomes syrupy again – 3 to 5 minutes.

Add the orange rind, rhubarb, cumin and ¼ teaspoon of the salt to the saucepan. Cover the pan and cook the mixture until the rhubarb is soft and has begun to lose its shape – about 15 minutes. Purée the mixture through a sieve.

While the rhubarb is cooking, preheat the grill. Rinse the fillets under cold running water and pat them dry with paper towels. Sprinkle the remaining salt and some pepper over the skinless side of the fillets. Place the fish skin side down on a baking sheet and brush the tops with the oil. Grill the fillets about 8.5 cm (3½ inches) below the heat source for 6 minutes, then turn the fillets skin side up and cook them for 2 minutes more. To test for doneness, insert a fork into a fillet at its thickest point; the flesh should be opaque all the way through.

Gently transfer the fillets to a serving platter, add the rhubarb sauce and garnish with the orange slices.

Grilled Freshwater Bream

Serves 4

Working time: about 30 minutes

Total time: 1 hour and 10 minutes

Calories 290

Protein 44g

Cholesterol 90mg

Total fat 12g

Saturated fat 1g

Sodium 360mg

2	freshwater bream (about 750 g/1½ lb each)	2
1 tbsp	virgin olive oil	1 tbsp
1 tsp	green peppercorns, crushed	1 tsp

	fresh rosemary sprigs	
	fresh thyme sprigs	
½ tsp	salt	½ tsp
	lemon wedges for garnish	

Remove the fins, scales and viscera, but not the head, from the bream. Wash the fish well under cold running water, then pat them dry with paper towels. Make two or three deep slashes in the sides of each bream. Rub the olive oil and the crushed peppercorns over the bream, then press sprigs of fresh rosemary and thyme into the slashes. Season the fish with the salt.

Put the fish on a dish, cover them and let them stand for 30 minutes.

Heat the grill to high. Place the fish in a fish grill, or on a rack in the grill pan. Grill for 4 to 5 minutes on each side, until the flesh flakes easily. Garnish with lemon wedges and serve immediately.

Alternatively, the bream can be baked in an oven preheated to 200°C (400°F or Mark 6): place the fish in an ovenproof dish and bake uncovered for 25 minutes until cooked.

Suggested accompaniment: curly endive and orange salad.

Trout Stuffed with Kumquats and Spring Greens

Serves 8

Working time: about 45 minutes

Total time: about 1 hour and 15 minutes

Calories
290

Protein
24g

Cholesterol
50mg

Total fat
18g

Saturated fat
4g

Sodium
280mg

2.5 kg	trout (or sea trout or salmon), scaled and filleted, skin left on	**5 lb**
2	garlic cloves, finely chopped	**2**
2 tbsp	fresh lemon juice	**2 tbsp**
¾ tsp	salt	**¾ tsp**
	freshly ground black pepper	
2	medium leeks, trimmed, split, washed thoroughly to remove any grit, and thinly sliced	**2**
30 g	unsalted butter	**1 oz**
2 tbsp	safflower oil	**2 tbsp**
1½ tsp	fresh thyme, or ½ tsp dried thyme	**1½ tsp**
125 g	fresh kumquats, thinly sliced and seeded	**4 oz**
350 g	spring greens, washed, stemmed and chopped	**12 oz**
45 g	dry breadcrumbs	**1½ oz**

Run your fingers over the fillets to locate any small bones; using tweezers, carefully pull out the bones. Rinse fillets under cold water and pat dry with paper towels. Rub with the garlic, lemon juice, ½ teaspoon of salt and some pepper. Set fillets aside while you prepare the stuffing.

Preheat the oven to 190°C (375°F or Mark 5). Put the butter and 1 tablespoon of the oil in a large, heavy frying pan over medium heat. When the butter has melted, add the leeks and thyme; cook, stirring occasionally, for 5 minutes. Stir in the kumquats and cook for 2 minutes more. Add the spring greens, the remaining salt and some more pepper. Cook the mixture until

the spring greens are wilted and tender – 5 to 7 minutes. Stir in the breadcrumbs and remove the pan from the heat.

Lay one of the fish fillets skin side down in a large, lightly oiled baking dish. Spread the greens-kumquat mixture over the fillet. Lay the remaining fillet skin side up on the stuffing. Brush the remaining oil over the top of the fish.

Bake the assembly until the fillets are opaque and the filling is hot – 25 to 30 minutes. Transfer the fish to a serving platter, slice, and serve.

Suggested accompaniment: baked potatoes with chives.

Useful weights and measures

Weight Equivalents

Avoirdupois		Metric
1 ounce	=	28.35 grams
1 pound	=	254.6 grams
2.3 pounds	=	1 kilogram

Liquid Measurements

$^1/_4$ pint	=	$1^1/_2$ decilitres
$^1/_2$ pint	=	$^1/_4$ litre
scant 1 pint	=	$^1/_2$ litre
$1^3/_4$ pints	=	1 litre
1 gallon	=	4.5 litres

Liquid Measures

1 pint	= 20 fl oz	= 32 tablespoons
$^1/_2$ pint	= 10 fl oz	= 16 tablespoons
$^1/_4$ pint	= 5 fl oz	= 8 tablespoons
$^1/_8$ pint	= $2^1/_2$ fl oz	= 4 tablespoons
$^1/_{16}$ pint	= $1^1/_4$ fl oz	= 2 tablespoons

Solid Measures

1 oz almonds, ground = $3^3/_4$ level tablespoons
1 oz breadcrumbs fresh = 7 level tablespoons
1 oz butter, lard = 2 level tablespoons
1 oz cheese, grated = $3^1/_2$ level tablespoons
1 oz cocoa = $2^3/_4$ level tablespoons
1 oz desiccated coconut = $4^1/_2$ tablespoons
1 oz cornflour = $2^1/_2$ tablespoons
1 oz custard powder = $2^1/_2$ tablespoons
1 oz curry powder and spices = 5 tablespoons
1 oz flour = 2 level tablespoons
1 oz rice, uncooked = $1^1/_2$ tablespoons
1 oz sugar, caster and granulated = 2 tablespoons
1 oz icing sugar = $2^1/_2$ tablespoons
1 oz yeast, granulated = 1 level tablespoon

American Measures

16 fl oz	=1 American pint
8 fl oz	=1 American standard cup
0.50 fl oz	=1 American tablespoon

(*slightly smaller than British Standards Institute tablespoon*)

0.16 fl oz	=1 American teaspoon

Australian Cup Measures

(*Using the 8-liquid-ounce cup measure*)

1 cup flour	4 oz
1 cup sugar (crystal or caster)	8 oz
1 cup icing sugar (free from lumps)	5 oz
1 cup shortening (butter, margarine)	8 oz
1 cup brown sugar (lightly packed)	4 oz
1 cup soft breadcrumbs	2 oz
1 cup dry breadcrumbs	3 oz
1 cup rice (uncooked)	6 oz
1 cup rice (cooked)	5 oz
1 cup mixed fruit	4 oz
1 cup grated cheese	4 oz
1 cup nuts (chopped)	4 oz
1 cup coconut	$2^1/_2$ oz

Australian Spoon Measures

	level tablespoon
1 oz flour	2
1 oz sugar	$1^1/_2$
1 oz icing sugar	2
1 oz shortening	1
1 oz honey	1
1 oz gelatine	2
1 oz cocoa	3
1 oz cornflour	$2^1/_2$
1 oz custard powder	$2^1/_2$

Australian Liquid Measures

(*Using 8-liquid-ounce cup*)

1 cup liquid	8 oz
$2^1/_2$ cups liquid	20 oz (1 pint)
2 tablespoons liquid	1 oz
1 gill liquid	5 oz ($^1/_4$ pint)